Ninety-nine Da

Ninety-nine Days

Ninety-nine Days

The story of the Benjamins' Round Britain Sail

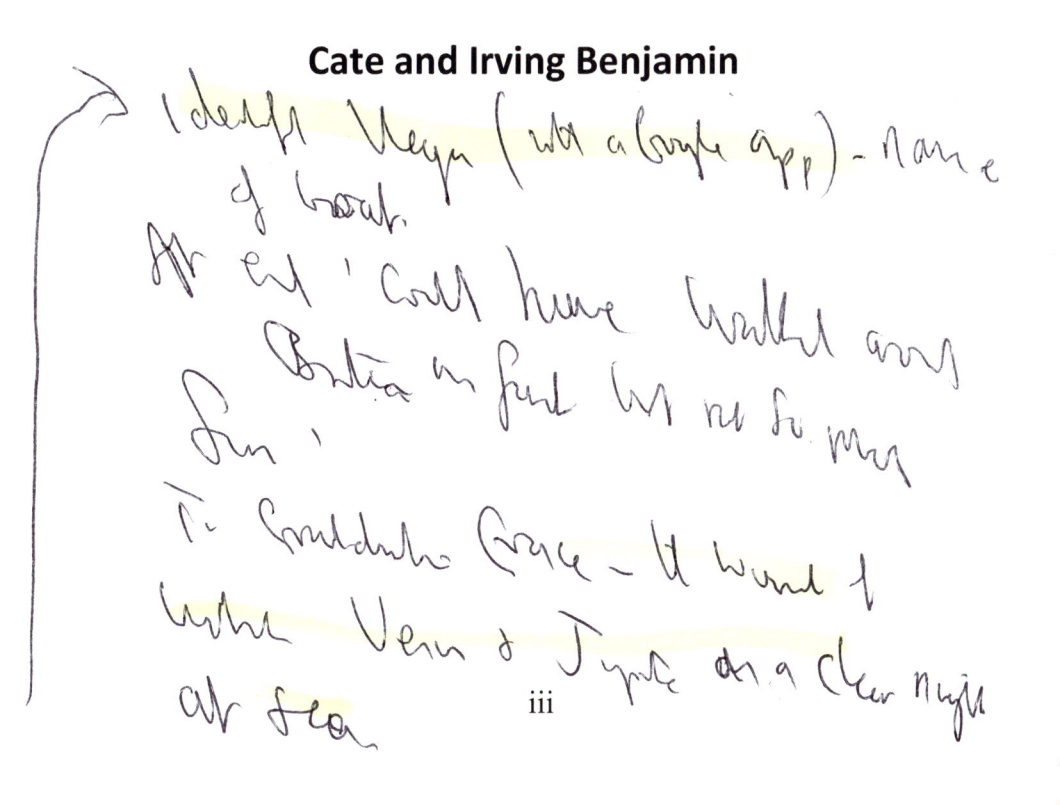

Cate and Irving Benjamin

Cate and Irving Benjamin

Copyright © 2020 by Irving Benjamin
All rights reserved. This book or any portion thereof
may not be reproduced or used in any manner whatsoever
without the express written permission of the publisher
except for the use of brief quotations in a book review.

Printed in the United Kingdom

First Printing, 2020

ISBN: 9798568434764

Imprint: Independently published

Kindle Direct Publishing

Ninety-nine Days

Dedication

This book is produced loving memory of Cate Benjamin,
who always believed it would happen.

All sales are in aid of *Pilgrims Hospices, Kent,*
with thanks for their inestimable support for both of us.

Cate and Irving Benjamin

Contents

Week 0 : D-Day-25 14
    Sat 21 April – 14 May 2012 14
    Dover boatyard 51: 7.07N 1:18.53E............................... 14

WEEK ONE 17
    16th-22nd May 17
    Dover to Plymouth 17

WEEK TWO 29
    May 23rd - 29th 29
    Plymouth to Kilmore Quay 29

WEEK THREE 43
    30th May- 5th June 43
    Kilmore Quay to Ardglass... 43

WEEK FOUR 53
    June 6th – 12th.. 53
    Ardglass to Ballycastle 53

WEEK FIVE 65
    June 13th- 19th 65
    Ballycastle (NI) to Oban (Scotland) 65

WEEK SIX 81
    20th – 26th June... 81
    Oban to Oban via Lochaline and Glasgow! 81

WEEK SEVEN 92
    27th June – 10th July 92
    Oban to Rum (via Glasgow).. 92

WEEK EIGHT **109**
    11th – 17th July 109
    Rum to Inverie 109

WEEK NINE **129**
    July 18th – 20th 129
    Inverie to Oban 129

WEEK TEN **134**
    24th-31st July 134
    Oban to Portree via Largs... 134

WEEK ELEVEN **142**
    1st – 7th August.. 142
    Portree to Wick via Orkney 142

WEEK TWELVE **160**
    8th – 14th August 160
    Wick to Whitby 160

WEEK THIRTEEN **174**
    15th – 22nd August 174
    Home strait – Whitby to Deal.. 174

Appendices **188**
    Biographies... 188
    Vega, the boat.. 189
    Victualling Vega... 191
    Index of places and people's names 192

Prologue: Benj

June 2003

"Can we sail everywhere?"

I will always remember these words from Cate as we motored slowly down towards our temporary mooring in the middle of the River Hamble. Hardly 'sailing', and my inexpert handling of the newly-purchased yacht *Vega* would scarcely inspire confidence in the possibility of travelling the world in our little craft. Nonetheless, those light-hearted words have always stayed with me, little though I could have dreamt then of the adventures we would share in the subsequent 16 years.

I had long harboured the desire to sail, since reading *'Swallows and Amazons'* from the local library in land-locked Salford, never having set eyes on an actual sailing boat. My first craft was *OBY*, a 12ft *Pacer* dinghy, purchased from one of my surgical colleagues after my appointment as Professor of Surgery at King's College Hospital, and I taught myself to sail her on St Mary's Reservoir in West London. My real introduction to 'big boat' sailing was passing a week long Day Skipper Course in the Solent, with my oldest friend David and his brother John, and friend Hugh. Thereafter the group of us chartered boats for a week in the West of Scotland or Croatia in the succeeding summers.

But it wasn't until some time after the death of my first wife Barbara, in 2000, that the notion of actually owning my own boat took root in my mind, and I set off, guided by my very experienced sailor brother-in-law Mark, to find a suitable craft. I had in mind my non-sailing grown up children, and felt that the answer might be a motor-sailer, which would offer a degree of live-aboard comfort that might entice them to share my enthusiasm. That was in fact never to be, but at around the same time I had become an 'item' with my now wife Cate, and so it was with her collaboration that *Vega* was identified as an ideal craft in Hamble Marina, and the bargain was struck. The details of *Vega*, an LM Vitesse 33, are in the Appendix, but she seemed a prefect boat for our purpose. Before I could make the delivery passage to her new home berth of Dover, helped by Mark and David, I had several trial runs in the Hamble, and it was on one such that in the balmy summer evening, coasting gently down the river, that Cate spoke the words that were to prove so prescient. We haven't sailed 'everywhere' but we've given it a jolly good shot in half a dozen countries over the last 16 years, and *'Ninety-nine Days'* is an account of our Biggest Adventure, sailing round (most of) Britain two-handed, far from a unique achievement, but something we could never have imagined back in 2003.

This account is based on the daily log entries and blog messages sent home *en route*, and to our surprise we learned at the Laying Up Supper of the Royal Cinque Ports Yacht Club in November of that year that we had been awarded the cup for the best log, as the members had been following our progress with interest.

However, before we describe the trip, Cate felt we should set the scene with a short account of our first ever unassisted passage together, a day sail from Dover to Ramsgate. My original version of this was written as a 'Confession' for an anthology of writing for the Royal Cinque Ports Yacht Club. However, when Cate read it she was quick to point out a number of differences of memory and interpretation in my account, and she added her own (much clearer) perspective on the event. The following therefore reflects a more accurate description of our first 'duo' passage, in the light of which the reader may wonder how we ever made it all the way round the coast of the UK only a few years later. Cate's amendments to my original description are clearly marked. Read on…

Benj's Confession
(With *addenda* by his wife Cate)

It was a perfect autumn morning. The early sun was warming the air, and a light breeze stirred the flags in the marina, setting the metal halyards of the moored yachts clanking musically. Squadrons of gulls wheeled noisily over the famous white cliffs. A perfect day for a sail.

This was to be our first trip together in *Vega,* our 33ft LM Vitesse deck saloon cruiser, since purchasing her in Hamble and moving her to Dover. The delivery cruise, by way of Brighton and Eastbourne, had been undertaken with two fellow sailors aboard as crew, but this time my wife and I would be on our own. There was a club "rally" (only two boats took part in fact) to Ramsgate, which seemed an ideal opportunity for us to get used to the local tides and navigation round the infamous boat-catching Goodwin Sands.

We motored out of the marina smoothly, made the mandatory call to Port Control for instructions, and left Dover Harbour via the eastern entrance, without interference from the frequent arrivals and departures of the cross-channel ferries. The sails were hoisted, and the diesel engine turned off, leaving only the delicious sound of our wake bubbling past the stern, and we settled back to enjoy the sail. We waved a greeting to our home as we passed Deal pier. Even though Cate had almost no sailing experience before this *It was actually our very first sail alone together,* we made the outward passage uneventfully, on a pleasant broad reach most of the way.

Well, that was until we had to take the sails down. He told me to take the wheel and go head-to-wind. I had had some practice on the tiller but not the wheel. No idea what I was doing, steering one way then over-correcting on the other. Him repeatedly shouting `HEAD TO WIND' as the sails and boom did their level best to throw him overboard. Me thinking, `It'll knock him overboard, he'll hit his head and drown and I'll be left on this stupid boat all by myself'. By now I am shaking from head to toe, weeping and hyperventilating.

Cate and Irving Benjamin

We successfully avoided the Goodwins, dropped our sails off Ramsgate harbour, and motored on admiring the magnificent terrace housing the Royal Temple Yacht Club towering above us, and feeling rather self-satisfied. I must admit however that after our entry to the marina our approach to the pontoon did cause some alarm to a party of motor-boaters who were happily lunching on their afterdeck *because HE changed his mind about where we were going at the last moment and I had fenders and warps out on the other side of the boat,* but we made it alongside with no damage and felt quite pleased with ourselves *NOT! He stepped off to go and visit the other club boat and I went below and took a large slug of whisky straight from the bottle.*

After enjoying a warm sun-drenched lunch relaxing in the cockpit, we set off for home, and it was there that I made my first *FIRST!!???* major error. We stowed the warps and fenders, motored out into the Channel and turned head-to-wind. I left Cate to steer *who had just about figured out a modicum of control on the wheel* while I went to the mast to hoist the mainsail. Cate spotted a large ferry well away to the east, and pointed it out to me. I looked up briefly from the halyard and said: "Oh, don't worry about him: the ferries don't come into Ramsgate any more, he must be heading down the Channel to Dover". *He was behind the sail and couldn't see the approaching ship, and I had my eyes glued to the compass trying to keep the boat on the right heading and wasn't looking.* This was a dangerously wrong assumption, as we discovered when we heard five loud blasts from the (now not-so-distant) ferry, which was bearing down on us in a direct line for the harbour entrance. I quickly returned to the cockpit yelling 'GOING ABOUT' and motored us at top speed out of the shipping channel, where we *HE!* waved apologetically to the passing ferry *(I ducked down below)* as the huge ship entered Ramsgate harbour. We sailed home to Dover, safe but chastened.

Lessons learned: don't make assumptions about where other boats are going, and don't b****r about near the harbour entrance! *Oh, and DON'T EXPECT CREW TO KNOW WHAT THEY'RE DOING WHEN THEY HAVEN'T A CLUE!*

So that was our 'maiden' voyage together in *Vega*. Our first actual cruise round the UK started in 2007, accompanied by a variety of additional shipmates, but came to an abrupt halt in the West of Scotland, when Cate found the first sign of the breast cancer which was to change our lives for the following years. Cate returned to London for surgery, chemotherapy and radiotherapy, and instead of going 'over the top' we took the shortcut through the Caledonian Canal and 'parked' *Vega* in Inverness until the Spring of 2008. Various combinations of crew then joined us on the way down the east coast as far as Lowestoft, after which we turned left and headed for the Netherlands, where *Vega* was berthed for the next two years, with regular outings for both of us by way of the Dover-Dunquerque ferry, not finally returning to Dover Marina until 2010. So technically our first (partial) circumnavigation actually took 3 years, unlike the second one, which lasted -

***Ninety-nine Days** ...*

Week 0 : D-Day-25
Sat 21 April – 14 May 2012
Dover boatyard 51: 7.07N 1:18.53E

Sat 21 April
Thirty days until our planned departure for the 2012 Round Britain Jolly. Life has been too chaotic (aka, normal) so the Benjamins are, as ever, behind time.

Cate, Leigh (Cate's son) and I watched Vega lifted out onto the hard in Dover last Monday, and I spent a day scraping barnacles off the saildrive in a cold breeze, and bought the antifoul for next week's rubbing and painting. A lot to do, and our lives seem to be busier than ever. I have, however, at least worked out a proposed passage plan for the whole trip (I know, *'the best laid schemes o' mice and men'* etc) using PCPlanner and C-Map cartridges (which I need to have updated before we go – note to self).

Onwards and upwards!

Sun 22 April
Waking to a beautiful sunny Sunday morning. Ideal for antifouling/polishing ...

Looking after 6 year old grand-daughter Grace today so not sure how much of the above will get done. At least my lingering head cold seems better so far, in part thanks to coffee in bed from angel wife! *(Note to self - it's impossible to measure, many years in retrospect, how essential such ministrations have been to the pursuit of our goals!)*

Tue 24 April
Leigh and Benj made the most of a few hours without rain to scrub the hull ready for antifouling, painted rust primer on the starboard side of the keel, and sprayed first coat of hard antifoul on the saildrive and prop. There was a hose pipe ban in SE Britain at the time, but our task was made possible by the local water authority re-defining some of the

authorised uses of a hose to include 'washing decks', which I locally defined as extending to below the waterline! However, it still needed a major effort as the marina tap is three long hose-lengths away, and even with our joints the nozzle only just reached the bow! Anyway, phase one done, which is especially fortunate as heavy rain is forecast for the next two days! 20 days to go!

Friday 27 April
The Good, The Bad and the Downright Careless!.
The good news and the bad news: two long solo sessions in breaks between the torrential rain mean that Vega is antifouled (Seajet Blue, 1 can @£65), the saildrive reassembled and spray antifouled (Blakes - half the price of International) and re-anoded, and topsides cleaned and polished and (in my opinion) looking really good! Second major achievement was at last to fix the furling gear which has bugged us every year as we hoist the Genoa. It looks as if two grubscrews had never been correctly located when the standing rigging was replaced several years ago (not by me), resulting in an unstable foil round the forestay, resulting in several fraught sessions lying flat out on the foredeck freeing the jammed foresail, invariably in a Force 5 wind and rough sea. Today's repair should make life easier. (But did it? Read on…)

HOWEVER: having achieved all the painting without a single splash, while descending from the boat I managed to lose my grip on a plastic box containing an old tin of Plastimo Navy antifoul, which landed and opened onto the freshly cleaned teak sole of the cockpit, and splashed over the GRP of the cockpit seats and starboard side coaming. With much cursing at my own stupidity, I managed to get the box off the boat (down the ladder in the wind - the cause of the accident) and wash/scrub as much as possible off, leaving only a few stains. The (formerly) gleaming white GRP of the cockpit is another matter, and is still defaced despite much immediate scrubbing. I have posted for advice on various sailing fora, and will have to revisit (when the rain stops) with bleach (?), paint stripper (?) and much trepidation. Sadly not the end to a perfect day.

Anyway, the upside is that we re-launch next week (Tuesday 1st May) with ONLY 13 DAYS TO GO!!!

Sunday 6 May
Progress??

Much water under the bridge but not much under the keel since last posting. After spending some hours removing most of the blue antifoul stain last Monday, Vega was relaunched on Tuesday 2nd, only to discover no water flowing through the engine. In view of the critical lack of time until D(eparture)-Day, we called the excellent Mick & Paul Motors to come and diagnose both that and our recalcitrant outboard, which they duly did while Benj was off yomping across Dartmoor for half the week on a London Deanery Leadership Course! *(Cue much mockery from Cate.)* Cate and Benj sped up to Whitstable on Saturday to get the missing outboard impeller (and enjoy a nice seafood lunch *en passent*) and today Benj played Bb Baritone in the Betteshanger Brass Band[1] concert on the Deal Memorial Bandstand, then returned home to do a bit of minor mainsail stitchery while Cate looked after 6-year-old grand-daughter Gracie. Still MUCH to do, and it's now D-Day minus 8!

Tuesday 8 May
Back in Wellington Dock

Well, at least we're back on our own berth, the wonderful M&P have fixed the impeller, and Cate and I have put the sails on. Late evening working aboard for Benj, deflating and stowing dinghy, scrubbing decks, sorting some chaotic electrics, and returning the provisioning boxes to Taverners for Cate to check and re-stock. Not too confident of making Monday 14th (SIX DAYS!) for departure, especially with a full day's Deanery work on Thursday and grandson Oliver's 18th Birthday party in London on Sunday, but we're still trying! In the end it may be the weather that thwarts us, as it's still blowing a hooley at present.

Monday 14 May
Boat provisioned, cleaned (more or less), gas/electrics/plotter/VHF etc etc all checked - and wind Beaufort 6 today!!! Will we ever get away? Maybe tomorrow, maybe next day …

---

[1] A piece of history this: Benj and a substantial number of colleagues subsequently broke away from the Betteshanger Colliery Brass Band due to personality clashes, and now plays euphonium in Deal Brass Academy, enjoying in 2019 their 6th successful year as an independent band. http://www.dealbrass.org

WEEK ONE
16th-22nd May
Dover to Plymouth

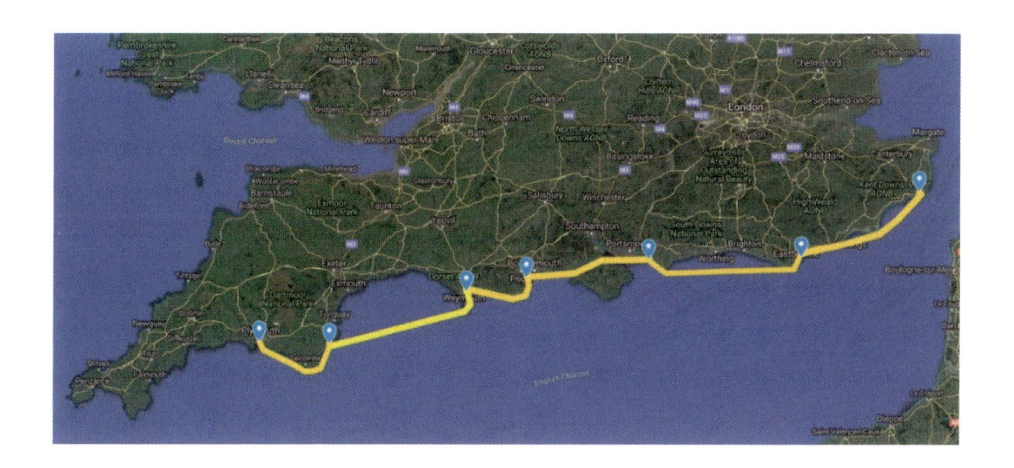

Cate and Irving Benjamin

Day 1 Wednesday 16th May
Dover to Sovereign Harbour Eastbourne
`N50:47'.34 E00:19'.90`

Off at last! Left home with enough extra baggage to sink let alone fill our little ship, and with Leigh's help loaded the lot. Along with our new very expensive folding bikes and our provisions it's just as well we left the cat behind because there's definitely no room to swing one.

Left Wellington dock at 0950, hoisted the main inside the outer harbour and set off to the SW motor-sailing with a 10knot wind on the nose, into what the forecast had promised would be light winds, decreasing during the day. So much for weather forecasts: the wind steadily increased to 23k (on the nose of course), with a steep and unpleasant sea with a short fetch which slammed us down regularly with a shuddering bang! Visits to the heads were interesting, with Cate defying gravity to head-butt the ceiling and then landing with a crunch on her coccyx! We eventually gave up with the sail (even dropping it was a bit of an adventure) and round about Bexhill-on-Sea we headed inshore for some lesser waves, dodging many lobster pots hidden by the swell. So our pleasant 8 hour passage ended 10 hours later in Eastbourne. Through the lock, manned 24/7, and into a quiet and sheltered berth (£24). After a pint in the Sovereign Harbour Yacht Club - a large modern building with a very busy lounge bar - we retired to *Vega* and dined on Cate's excellent casserole, brought in the pressure cooker: it will give us a good meal tomorrow too, when we arrive (hopefully) in Chichester after the next promised calm passage.

Ninety-nine Days

Cate and Irving Benjamin

Day 2 Thu 17 May Eastbourne to Chichester
Sparkes Marina, Chichester
Lat: 50:46.86N Lon: 0:56.06W

After yesterday's worse-than-advertised weather, we started the day with some uncertainty. The Met Office spoke of a start with SE 3-4, freshening to 5-6 *'later'*, and it was the 'later' we were unsure of with the prospect of a 50+nM passage. We set off at 0930 (suitable for the tides) with a fallback plan that if the F5-6 arrived as we were close to *Brighton*, we could dive in and hole up there, with the possible positive side effect of some retail therapy for Cate. We rounded *Beachy Head* with great views of the old and new lighthouses, and as we passed that point on the passage we made the decision to press on, in the belief that it was not likely to be as bad as yesterday. In the end we had a hearty motor trip with a vigorous following sea, and good to fair tide for the first 7 hours.

The tide changed on cue, and we had to gun the engine to get through the narrow Looe Channel past *Selsey Bill* to beat a 4knot tide against us. We navigated the *Chichester* harbour bar (sand bar, not drinking bar for those who don't know) with a sense of *deja vu*: I (Benj) have only been up this channel twice before. The first time we lost a prop and went aground for the night, and the second we limped in as a port of refuge when I broke four ribs on passage. This time it was much better, with only our guard rail snagged on the bow anchor of a Beneteau as we battled to berth in a 20+ knot easterly in a narrow marina. Safely tucked up (not where we should have been), and paid our 35 of your British pounds to MDL Marinas for the night. *(I think MDL stands for Maximum Dosh Levied.)* Dined on Cate's casserole for second and last night, and off to make a plan for tomorrow - Poole possibly.

Day 3 Fri 18 May
Chichester to Poole

Ninety-nine Days

Lat: 50:40.93N Lon: 1:56.96W

There's a sailors' saying, that the weather forecast is too inaccurate to rely on but too important to ignore. So we're keeping track of how often the Met Office gets the wind and weather wrong. Three out of three so far: today there was for all useful purposes NO wind (forecast 3-4 SE) so another day motoring. Not only that but there was 'nothing to see, folks, move along there' because of the fog which descended (that one was correctly forecast) as we left the western Solent. In fact the only wind we had all day was in the marina, necessitating a very tricky springing manoeuvre to get off our berth! Once down the harbour channel and over the bar (thankfully at high water) we headed for the Forts, passing close to No Man's Land Fort (picture) and westward along the coast of the Isle of Wight. Passing Cowes we had fun dodging a serious racing fleet with spinnakers all round us and crew lined up along the weather rails. We would have liked to take the Needles Passage to get some nice pics, but by then the fog had arrived and we settled for Hurst Narrows and then across Christchurch and Poole Bays in poor visibility. We entered Poole harbour avoiding the chain ferry and the Poole-Cherbourg ferry and berthed in the Town Quay Marina. I discovered that the further west you go the more expensive the fees - a staggering £41 here for a night!

Walk into town, visiting the chandlers and scoping out our evening's entertainment, then back for fish and chips aboard. On the quayside there was a car owners' rally, with a line-up of more Porsches than you could shake a big stick at! The Antelope in King St had a live band - the JuJu Men - with 'Retro R&B' and we settled down for a couple of hours of music on a comfy sofa, before heading home for an early night. Tomorrow's plan is a later departure (allowing for Shopping) to catch the tide round Anvil Point for Weymouth.

Day 4 - 19 May
Poole to Weymouth
Lat: 50:36.57N Lon: 2:26.58W

Had a morning shopping and some light boat maintenance, and then refuelled in Poole and set off at 1300. We gave the two headlands and their overfalls (Anvil Point and St Abb's Head - see Old Harry Rocks picture) a wide berth but were still buffeted a bit. Again the wind was wrong for any but a very wide tacking sail, so it was another day motoring, arriving at Weymouth Harbour 1800.

We called the Harbour Master to try for a berth outside his office, and the Royal Dorset Yacht Club, but were directed to the left bank - The Cove - where we were rafted against *Maxi Miss*, with a young crew who were leaving the following morning. We remained uncertain whether to have our 'rest day' in Weymouth, depending on the dreaded weather forecast, so kept our options open and booked for one night.

We visited the RDYC which we found massively changed since my last visit: they have relocated upstairs from the small bar I remember, and now have a bar/lounge/dining room/decked garden which would not be out of place in Homes and Gardens magazine. We arrived as the members were assembling for a formal Commodore's and Former Commodores' Dinner (maybe we should have one at RCPYC - I can only think of a couple of ex-Comms I wouldn't want to sit next to!) and we enjoyed a beer (Doom Bar for me) in the lounge as they sat down. There was a minute's silence for three young fishermen who were lost yesterday off the coast nearby when their boat sank for no apparent reason, leaving an undeployed liferaft aboard. There were floral tributes and notes along the harbour wall. Back to the boat for a super steak and salad supper cooked aboard. I had pre-loaded my mobile hard drive with films and other old programmes, and we watched the very first episode of The Sopranos on Cate's laptop before retiring. (Cate has just corrected this - SHE watched, and I fell asleep!)

Day 5 May 20 –
Weymouth to Dartmouth
Lat: 50:21.02N Lon: 3:34.25W

A snap decision to leave and catch the tide round *Portland Bill* followed by hurried preparation and a departure at 0945. It is VERY important to arrive at the Bill at slack water (4 hours after HW Portland), or you get caught up in one of the most frantically confused tidal races in the UK. We made it exactly on time, and giving the headlands a healthy wide berth we were on a single course of 260° for *Dartmouth*, 55nM distant. Once the tide had turned with us (1300) we were - *Hallelujah!* - able to sail. Full sail, close reach, making 6-7k in 14k NW wind. At last the forecast was right, but sadly it didn't last long enough. By 1500 it had veered north and died away to 8k, and we were down to 3k boat speed, which would have given us an ETA of after dark. So... back on with the Iron Mainsail and onwards to *Dartmouth*.

After the loss of the fishermen 2 days ago, there has been more awful news coming over the VHF - a missing diver not far from the *Dart*. A prolonged search was under way, but sadly was abandoned shortly after 1700, signalled on the radio as a *Mayday Silence Finis* - very doleful words to hear. Anyway, we arrived at the magnificent entrance of the *Dart* at 1730, dropped the main and called *Darthaven* Marina for a berth. This marina has also changed since my last visit, and now has very posh electronic gates of gleaming glass and chrome. After 'Evening Prayers'[2] we walked up the hill to *Kingswear* village and down to the *Royal Dart YC* to sign in and have a beer, then back to the boat past the pretty retro GWR station of the steam line to *Paignton*, a trip which Cate and I had enjoyed in 2003! Dined aboard and typed up the blog, and retired at midnight, planning our 'rest day' tomorrow.

---

[2] Because our Deal home is a converted 17th Century Baptist Chapel, we have always termed our sundowners (ca. 1800) 'Evening Prayers', and this has continued to be the traditional terminology when seaborne. And even when ashore. Cheers!

Ninety-nine Days

Day 6 Mon 21 May
'Rest Day' Kingswear/Dartmouth

Gentle rise to a magnificent day - almost like it was summer - and to use the splendid 5* facilities of *Darthaven* Marina, then across on the unique push-pull ferry to the Dartmouth side for breakfast at the equally unique *Alf Resco*: Benj of course had to have the Big Alf - all the usual full English plus Devon Hog Pudding (like a white pudding) - washed down with orange juice freshly squeezed before your eyes. With full bellies we had no need for lunch thereafter.

We then separated to our respective tours of the shops/sights of Dartmouth. We separately explored St Saviour's Church, a 14th Century gem, with magnificent carved and painted stone pulpit and incredible carved wooden reredos screen, with hidden 'green men'. The oak door with iron bindings has been carbon dated to show it was probably part of the original church, dating to the 1200s. Met up again for a beer at the *Crab and Bucket* on the quayside, and Benj returned on the ferry to rest his back, which had unfortunately been playing up since yesterday. Cate very sensibly found him an osteopath, in view of all the physical activities to come, but he adopted his usual 'leave it alone' policy. Fortunately, a couple of hours' rest produced some improvement, and we later made the ferry crossing again for our pre-booked

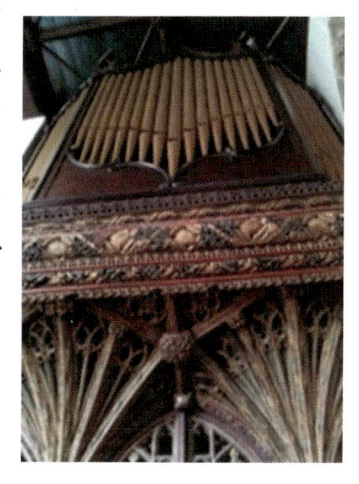

25

evening meal at the famous *Cherub*: this ancient pub had been lucky to escape a serious fire 2 years ago which severely damaged many of the town's old buildings. First-class meal - scallops, seabass, lamb's liver and pudding! Retired after our first 'rest day', ready for Plymouth on the morning tide.

Ninety-nine Days

Day 7 Tue 22 May
Dartmouth to Plymouth
Lat: 50:21.78N Lon: 4:10.03W

Sometimes life for a sailor carries some simple delights. Today before leaving the marina (Benj) bought 4.5 metres of thick and 4.5 metres of thin bungee cord to remake our elasticated sail tie, which has been deteriorating for several years now with no impetus to mend it: short trips don't leave time for all those little maintenance jobs, but on this long the Skipper's resolve was to catch up on the 'housework'. Anyway, we left as planned on the 1000 tide in wall-to-wall blue sky, (hairdy Scot Benj in shorts, S African Cate bundled up warm) enjoying what summer boating should be like for the first time. Motoring (again) but this time on a calm sea with clear views as we left the lovely River Dart, rounded Start Point, and headed west for Plymouth. Once we cleared the fishing-pot area with need for constant vigilance and frequent course alterations, we saw hardly another vessel for many miles, until the yachts in and out of Plymouth Sound began to appear.

By 1430 we were past the well-concealed mouth of the beautiful River *Yealm* (sorry we didn't have time for a visit), rounding the Mewstone, and shaping a course for the *Plymouth Sound* breakwater. I had planned to go via *The Bridge*, a good shortcut past *Drake's Island*, but as it was just past low water this did not seem a good idea - there's at least one area of 0.3m at low tide - so we followed the deep water fairway to the east of Drake and made Mayflower Marina at 1530. Pleasingly, Mayflower is a member of the TransEurope group, so as a Dover berth-holder we get a 50% discount: yeehah! - only £15 for the night!

After a cuppa we set off on the bus for the city, where we had a wander in the centre and then across Plymouth Hoe, past Smeaton's Tower (which we had ascended on our previous trip) and along the sea wall to the Royal Plymouth Corinthian YC, where we enjoyed a beer overlooking the racing in the harbour. Another short walk took us to the notorious Barbican, quiet at this early hour, though beset with numerous derelicts, some of them perceptibly drunk in charge of young infants - not a pretty sight. Hunger overcame us and we enjoyed one of the best Thai meals we have had in The Thai House in Notte Street, winner 'Devon's Best Thai Restaurant' and similar awards. In view of the rather long walk from the road to the marina we opted for a taxi home for £7, and had our nightcaps in Jolly Jack's, a lively bistro on the marina, well worth a visit.

WEEK TWO
May 23rd - 29th
Plymouth to Kilmore Quay

Cate and Irving Benjamin

Day 8 Wed 23 May
Plymouth to Falmouth (Mylor Yacht Haven)
Lat: 50:10.74N Lon: 5:03.14W

A mixed day of good and bad. The best was the weather - beautiful warm sun all day - and the opportunity to get our first decent sail. We left Plymouth as planned, this time taking the 'shortcut' through The Bridge, which looked frighteningly narrow and potentially shallow, but was a good route, as advised by Tom Cunliffe. (I haven't mentioned before that I have relied on "Uncle Tom"'s writings in the Shell Channel Pilot both for their sound advice and the wry humour all yachtsmen have grown to know and love: how he will be missed when anno domini catches up with him!)

Leaving the Sound we turned SW round Start Point and shaped a course to Falmouth with no waypoint for 45miles! As the wind was about due west we were faced with yet another long day on the iron mainsail, or a very long tack out to the south, allowing a few hours good sailing in 10-14k of wind before having to point towards our target. Needless to say we chose the latter, and had a very enjoyable and worthwhile diversion for the next two hours, close-hauled on a starboard tack, passing within a mile of the Eddystone Light, before turning head to wind on a four hour engine slog to Falmouth entrance.

There was entertainment during our sail from naval vessels HMS Kent and Lancaster on live firing manoeuvres. (Kent is a vessel 'adopted' by our club, Royal Cinque Ports Yacht Club, during a visit while I was Commodore.)

Ninety-nine Days

Once we reached *Falmouth* the 'bad' of the day started. We had difficulty contacting Falmouth Yacht Haven, and eventually were directed to a 'vacant' berth (which was not), manoeuvred very badly in trying to find even a rafted slot, and had to be fended off (thanks, Cate, yet again) and eventually gave up making further radio contact, and left. We tried Pendennis Marina, with equal lack of result and decided to head back into Carrick Roads and up to Mylor Yacht Haven. Could we raise them on the VHF? Could we *b*****y*! So we made our way there anyway, heading into a blinding low western sun to find the narrow buoyed channel, weaving our way through a Wednesday evening racing fleet of RS4000s and Lasers, to find an alongside berth with no authority. Our neighbour said he had found himself in the same position (and he is a berth-holder displaced from his rightful slot), so here we are as I type - after Evening Prayers - overnighting in a glorious evening light in a quiet creek without power or access to the bar, but probably free, so we can't complain! Sorry though to have missed the chance to meet up with Denise (my former PA) and husband Terry. Will have to wait until next year, when we may spend a longer time than we have had on this cruise exploring the glories of the West Country. Off now to heat up our pork and lentils.

Cate and Irving Benjamin

Day 9 Thursday 24 May
Falmouth to Newlyn
Lat: 50:06.19N Lon: 5:32.58W

Cate stayed abed while Benj slipped the berth at 0750 to catch the tide round The Lizard, in a light haze which soon burnt off to a full sunny day with wall-to-wall blue sky. I thought our wind instrument must have failed as it registered zero for the first time, but it became quickly apparent that that was an accurate reading, and one which persisted all day. So we motored along happily for six hours, clearing The Lizard's notorious overfalls by a safe 3M, and taking alternate watches, one hour on one hour off, avoiding dozens of fishing pots. Difficult decisions awaited regarding the need to refuel (I should have done it in Falmouth) for the long haul to Padstow next day: Penzance has fuel on the quay, but you can only get to it close to HW (which would be 1800), while Newlyn can provide diesel, but only in jerry cans from the Harbour Master. We tried to raise either port by VHF and by mobile phone, but with no response, so we made a snap decision and entered the very busy fishing harbour at Newlyn at 1330. A long trek found the HM office (but no HM) and eventually a place to buy fuel. I emptied 20L from our spare jerry can into the tank, and trekked back again for a refill, which I carted down to the pontoon on our folding trolley and filled up with that too. A bit of a slog, but that would give us enough fuel for at least 48 hours motoring if needed.

The next and more tricky dilemma was how to achieve the passage to Padstow (60+ miles) so as to avoid foul tide round Land's End and to arrive at the dreaded DOOM BAR (like the beer) at *Padstow* harbour close to high water. Actually whichever way you do it the sums don't quite add up, so compromises are needed. The other factor is that while the weather is lovely today and set fair for tomorrow, by Saturday it is supposed to be seriously sh***y, so we need to get to Padstow and hole up there waiting for the long passages to Wales and then to Ireland. After much head scratching, pencil rubbing out, and a word with the coxwain of the RNLI here in Newlyn, I decided to leave at 2200 for our first night sail of the voyage. Cate had gone to stock up on provisions and we prepared tortellini al' arrabiata (as you will read, we know how to live well aboard *Vega*) and rested up for the departure. The rest will be a story for another day.

Cate and Irving Benjamin

Day 9 into 10 - 24/25 May
Newlyn to Padstow
Lat: 50:34.52N Lon: 4:56.94W

Armed with the best information I could get and seasoned with a pinch of guesswork and a large dose of optimism we finished our pasta and set off into the gathering dusk at 2125, nav lights on, and all set for a night's motoring with the objective of rounding Land's End without too much confused tidal race and the hope that we might make Padstow for the narrow tidal window needed to enter the locked harbour. A slim crescent moon gave no illumination to the water as again we strained our eyes for lobster pot markers, and in fact it became yellower and fainter as a night mist descended over us. Of course once it is properly dark, whether one hits a pot (or any other floater) is entirely in the lap of the gods, so all you can do is plough on into the unknown, singing, with the aforementioned optimism in your heart, so that's what we did. As the passage was going to be at least 10 hours, I proposed that I would take the dark hours as a long watch since Cate has effectively no night vision, and I would hopefully wake her at first light and get a bit of rest before the potentially tricky pilotage into *Padstow*. I did want us both to have rounded *Land's End* together so we did that just before midnight, waving goodbye to the most westerly point of England, and Cate went below leaving me to the solitude of the wheelhouse, with only Otto (our faithful Autohelm) and spells of the BBC World Service for company. I had the radar on all night and saw not a single blip, as we motored initially at 4.5k, gradually increasing by about 0300 to 6.5k as the tide turned with us. First light was about 0430, with a misty view of the glassy water, so I woke Cate with a coffee to take her watch until 0600, and I caught a welcome nap.

The entrance into *Padstow* was far from obvious, with a narrow channel down the Camel estuary and no clear indication of the harbour entrance. We passed the dreaded *Doom Bar*, having managed to arrive the necessary 1-2 hours before local High Water, because as the attached picture shows, it's almost all sandbanks and very little water at other times. We weren't able to raise the HM on VHF until we were almost at the entrance channel, and we got into the small pretty harbour as the mist burnt away under bright sun, and at 0745 we were rafted against two other yachts against the harbour wall. The others left shortly after, so we slipped into their place against the stone harbour wall. That of course meant constant vigilance and regular readjustment of our lines with the rising and falling tide as the harbour gate opens and closes. Anyway, here we were, after our longest passage of the trip so far, and our first (and Cate's Maiden) night passage.

Days 10-11 25-26 May

Padstow rest days

Friday and Saturday in *Padstow* passed in unbroken sunshine, but accompanied by howling wind which continually blew black sand and grit from the harbour wall down on to our boat below, getting into every crevice on the deck, through the hatch, into the cockpit, onto our lunch, and onto all our bedding in the forepeak! Apart from that, and the continuous need to adjust our lines up and down to avoid arriving home from the shops or pub to find *Vega* suspended like a puppet, we passed a very pleasant two days' (largely wind-enforced) rest.

Padstow boasts shops, pubs and cafes aplenty, and the town was buzzing with visitors both days. Benj paid a visit to the National Lobster Hatchery - more interesting than it sounds - where he learned lots of things about the creatures, and saw how they rescue females who are pregnant ('berried'), keep them in a 'maternity ward', hatch and nurture the teeny lobsterlets until they are mature enough, and release them to replenish the stocks. Fascinating and well presented exhibits. *Padstow* (or Padstein, as it is known) is virtually owned by Rick Stein, and we visited his shop, his deli, his fish market, and (in passing) his seafood cookery school, and ate Friday supper at his Fish and Chip Shop (grilled mackerel and hake) and Saturday lunch at his Cafe (the best Seabass I have ever had) accompanied by *Chalky's Bite Ale*, named after Rick's dog, and fennel flavoured, at 5.8%. On Saturday afternoon Benj caught the Rugby Premiership Final (Quins 23 Tigers 16) at the *Old Ship Inn*, with lubrication from Sharp's Special, but sadly no *Doom Bar* available in the town where the actual Doom Bar is! We returned that evening for supper and some live music (not that good), and back to the boat to ready for next day's sailing. Cate retired and Benj sat up gradually letting the dock lines down until after midnight. Overall this was the highlight of our trip so far, relaxing in endless sunshine in a pretty harbour and town. *(Oops – Cate adds that my purchase of a new ship's broom for her forthcoming birthday rather dimmed the highlight! Sorry, darling.)*

Day 12 May 27
Padstow to Milford Haven
Lat: 51:42.41N Lon: 5:01.45W

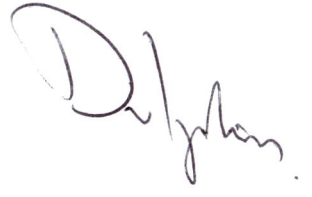

Departure time from *Padstow* is strictly limited by the harbour tidal gate opening, so we had planned ahead to leave on the first opening (0900), refuel on the harbour wall, and start our long passage to *Milford Haven* in Pembrokeshire. Refuelling was a bit of a nightmare, lying against a very rough outer harbour wall with metal ladders barely protected by rubber tyres, while the HM lowered the fuel pipe down to the boat 20ft below to fill up. 50 litres later, and with a full tank, we set off again over the *Doom Bar* and once we had cleared *Pendeen Head* we had a single course of 350°Mag for over 70 nM to the *Milford Haven* Approaches. Over a course of this length there is little point in making tide adjustments because there will be an offset to east and about the same to west before we strike land, so (motoring of course - after 2 days of F5-6 there was NO wind at all) we set the Autohelm and relaxed in the sun. In the late afternoon we spotted our first dolphins, who to our huge pleasure played around *Vega* for the best part of an hour.

Cate and I photographed and video'd away from the bow until our phone batteries ran dry, and still they played, twisting and turning under the bow, charging up at speed from behind and leaping singly or in twos and threes of elegant synchronised swimming.

The photos can hardly do the experience justice, but Cate was quick to upload some video to Facebook, where 'our' dolphins have been much admired by many FB friends. I attach one picture (from Cate's Samsung

Galaxy phone, which has a better camera than my digital SLR!), and also one of Cate doing the filming. (Spot the two 'deliberate' mistakes[3] in the picture of Cate at the bow by the way!) The dolphins returned an hour later for a repeat performance, and we were to comment on our next dolphin day (see later) that they seemed to arrive on the hour, give us a show, and then speed off into the distance. It was pitch dark when we finally made the enormous estuary harbour of *Milford Haven* (we forgot to fly a Welsh courtesy flag, I'm afraid, despite this being the land and indeed county – Pembrokeshire - of Cate's father) and navigating upriver in the dark through the huge docks and refineries was rather daunting, including being asked to make way by a Pilot Boat for a gigantic tanker leaving her berth. After several attempts we were glad to get a response from the Marina harbourmaster, and followed leading lights to a large lock which was open to free flow - a piece of good luck for us - and he actually came down to the pontoon to meet us in and take our line. It was now 2215 so we settled for a snack and retired after 14 hours and 75 Nautical Miles, which brought us up to 500nM since the start of our adventure. (PS: by the way, for those who don't know, a Nautical Mile is about 1.25 Statute Miles.)

[3.] Oh, the 'deliberate mistakes'? Cate is wearing no lifejacket at sea on the bow of the boat, and to make matters worse in her haste to get the dolphin pictures, is in her SLIPPERS! Tut!

Ninety-nine Days

Day 13 May 28
Cate's Birthday - rest day in Milford Haven

I was forced to confess that I hadn't thought ahead enough, nor had a close eye on the calendar, and to my eternal shame hadn't prepared anything for **Cate's Birthday**, so I was hoping against hope that I would find a suitable gift in what I had believed would be an attractive and interesting seaside town. Little did we suspect how little *Milford Haven* would have to offer! Given what little choice there was, Cate decided to spend the day exploring on her own, birthday shopping for a new mobile phone, and sight-seeing. We also had to find a nice Birthday Dinner for Cate, especially since the next leg was to be quite a long one, across *St George's Channel* to Ireland. A steep ascent up steps from the Marina led to the orderly grid of streets parallel to the harbour, as laid out by Sir Charles Greville in Nelson's time, consisting almost entirely of boarded-up shops, charity outlets, betting shops and closed hairdressers, with a couple of coffee shops and some uninviting pubs (including the *Nelson Inn*, renamed for the Admiral after his one visit to the town, during which he admired the actual harbour).

It did not take long to 'do' the town, and we stopped for coffee and cake overlooking the harbour, and chatted with the waitress about the sad and derelict state of the place, which makes our home town of *Deal* look like Manhattan. I could not fathom why a massive and presumably profitable oil terminal such as MH does not make any apparent investment in the town. One contributory cause, we later learned from a very informative visit to the town Museum, is that the oil terminal and refineries require a relatively small labour force, compared with a cargo or fishing port, and so there is little employment for the town coming from the harbour.

When we descended to the marina again it was a different story: on all sides there are coffee shops, restaurants and bijou shops selling designer labels, which is where all the visitors to the marina spend their dosh, not in the town. We also learned that the marina shopping area has become a magnet for visitors from as far away as *Cardiff*, while the town above withers on the vine. I'm afraid, lacking any alternative, we ended the day with a good meal at one of the marina restaurants, adding our contribution to the tourist dollar profits which entirely bypass the town. A very sad place indeed.

Ah, yes, the Birthday. A very sad and hurt Cate adds: "A postcard just didn't do it for me, so I simmered. Caught the bus into town on my own and bought my own bloody phone (Benj did later pay half)."

Sorry yet again, darling.

Day 14 May 29
Milford Haven to Kilmore Quay
Lat: 52:10.33N Lon: 6:35.90W

Refuelled and entered the lock at 0854 as arranged - you have to pre-book your locking out times - and left westwards with two other yachts, down the empty haven, rounding *St Ann's Head* at 1100. The day started dull and slightly drizzly, with NO wind! There are decisions to make on this course about the various rocky headlands and offshore islands with warnings in the almanac about severe overfalls and lost ships off *The Smalls*, a group of rocks whose name belies their importance as a hazard. To go round the *Smalls* adds on a good hour or so to the passage, so we decided that under the prevailing calm conditions we would steer a course inland between *The Smalls* and *Skomer Island*, and just live with the bumpy ride for a while. It turned out not to be too bad, though we rocked around quite a bit in the heavy swell. This passage crosses the ends of two Traffic Separation Schemes for BFSs[4] plying the Channel, and we used the radar to check and dodge the relative courses of a couple of BFSs and one large Irish Ferry. The rest of the passage was enlivened only by several more close encounters with dolphins, who again arrived regularly at 15 minutes past each hour in the middle part of the afternoon, so more photography and video was of course indicated, and Cate again uploaded some good film to Facebook. The lovely mammals are so close you could lean out over the bow (we did) and touch their backs (we didn't), and it was a thrilling experience again.

---

[4] BFS = our local terminology for Big F***ing Ships

On the Irish side, there is another well-tried 'shortcut' inside rocks and shoals via *'St Patrick's Bridge'*, a narrow channel which saves several nMs. We had used this route before in 2007, and navigated our way through with ease. We made the entrance to *Kilmore Quay* (quite a tricky one) at 2000, after a passage of 69nM, bringing us to a total of 567 at the end of this second week. The smallish marina, shared with a large fishing fleet, has a unique method of access via the locked gate: the HM when we called in on VHF gave us a mobile phone number, which you have to call when outside the gate. This gives an acknowledgment beep, and if you're lucky on about the third go a yellow light comes on and the gate unlocks. The same system should open the door to the facilities ashore, but didn't, and the HM told us in the morning that the door to the building doesn't open in the evenings, so you have to use the public toilet next door if necessary (it wasn't). We cooked chicken in white sauce with a tin of *ackee* (a first and probably a last for both of us) and retired.

WEEK THREE

30th May- 5th June
Kilmore Quay to Ardglass

Day 15 Wed 30 May
Kilmore Quay to Arklow.
Lat: 52:47.39N Lon: 6:09.54W

We woke this morning to fog dense enough to obscure the harbour wall, making our departure for *Arklow* unlikely. We compared notes with a neighbouring yacht aiming to go the same way, and with advice from the HM. The problem would not be seeing our way past the shoal waters and through *St Patrick's Bridge* again, but the likelihood of getting caught up in the ropes of lobster pots, of which we were told there are about 3000 in these waters. As it looked like a non-sailing day, we made enquiries about the bus times (one per day) to *Wexford*, where we could do an afternoon's shopping and sight-seeing. We had a cooked breakfast aboard, purchased from the village shop. A walk up both ends of the small village showed pub/hotels either closed or in a state of renovation ready for the influx of visitors we were told would arrive in the summer. We visited the enormous and well-stocked chandler, and bought a new Admiralty Chart for East Ireland. Then, just as we were getting prepared for our bus trip, the fog magically lifted, leaving bright sun on a sparkling sea! So we quickly readied the boat and headed out, back through the *Bridge*, and set a course to round *Carnore Point* and northwards for Arklow.

On our previous passage this way in 2007, we had taken the inland route, between rather complicated sand banks, but I wasn't in the mood for difficult navigation so made a new set of waypoints to go outside the shoals, inside the huge *Tuskar Rock*, and (with more dolphins at 1415!) and on up the coast. Close to 1500, we were motoring at 7k, but the wind was now 10k+ on our port quarter, so I decided to set the sail, and soon we had the glorious sound of our wake and no engine, and were still cruising along at 7k under full Genoa alone. This lasted for almost two hours, but when the wind strengthened and moved further aft, I decided it was time for the Iron Mainsail again, and we motored on through a rather uncomfortable swell, to reach the approach to *Arklow* at about 1930. Cate steered us through the *Arklow Sailing Club*'s Wednesday evening race and into the entrance.

I remembered *Arklow* well from last time, and now re-read my 2007 log account of it. There is a tiny marina with hardly any room to manoeuvre inside, but mercifully also a pontoon outside on the *Avoca River* where visitors may berth alongside, and that's what we did. We decided to be lazy and find a Chinese takeaway, and as we walked past the returned racing crew they said the Sailing Club might be open. Indeed it was: a lovely little club house, still smelling of fresh paint and furniture, having been just re-built and opened one week earlier. We had a chat and a beer (my first Guinness in Ireland for the trip) and took the members' advice to try the *New Asian Harvest* for our meal, and we crossed the bridge over the *Avoca* and had an excellent Chinese meal in comfort, rather than a takeaway. We stopped again at the ASC and had another Guinness and some more amusing conversation with the members, before retiring at 2300. I must comment that my account in 2007 of what a dismal hole *Arklow* was bears no resemblance to what we met this time: there is now a riverside gated residential estate, a large shopping mall with cinema and supermarket, and maritime museum. What a contrast to *Milford Haven*, and I wondered if Wexford has been the beneficiary of EU development monies.

Day 16 Thu 31 May
Arklow to Dunlaoghaire[5]
Lat: 53:18.16N Lon: 6:07.68W

This was to be a fairly civilised 45nM trip so we left with the good north-going tide at 1300 and made the entrance to *Dublin Bay* and the massive 820 berth marina of *Dun Laoghaire* at 1800 after a cloudy and drizzly motor trip. We deployed the radar some of the way as light fog descended. Having experienced the bizarre method of gate access in *Kilmore Quay* we were now fingerprinted (right and left index fingers) - a highly effective method with no numbers to forget - for access into the marina and all facilities. We enjoyed Evening Prayers at the right time for once, and walked into the small town for a recce. We found a good pub with free WiFi and also a Pizza takeaway, which we enjoyed aboard and retired, planning to visit the fleshpots (*Cate: "Speak for yourself!"*) of Dublin Town for the next day or two.

---

[5] Pronounced "Dun Leery", for those who don't know.

Ninety-nine Days

Days 17-19   Fri-Sun 1-3 June
Dublin Days

Friday. Showered on a barge at our end of the pontoons, thus saving a 400m walk to the main facilities, then used the excellent laundry facilities in the marina, and took the DART into *Dublin* for lunch (indifferent meal from a bad choice of pub in *Temple Bar*), then shopping etc. We would have liked to go to the *Abbey Theatre* but it was fully booked, so the evening's entertainment was a visit to the cinema for *Prometheus in 3D*: Cate voted it a good movie, despite being stressed throughout and just avoiding screaming during the goriest bits!

Saturday. We had spotted in a local paper that this Bank Holiday weekend there was a music festival with one of our favourite bands - *Hypnotic Brass Ensemble*, an eight-piece brass group from Chicago - playing, as well as better known groups such as *Left Field* (and lesser known ones like *Holy Fuck*) so we called Ticketmaster and booked! A combination of DART, tram and a very long walk got us to *Kilmainham Royal Hospital* grounds, where we enjoyed a good afternoon's fun and music despite increasing drizzle. *Hypnotic Brass Ensemble* were absolutely awesome, with the extra treat of meeting the band afterwards and chatting in the Press tent. Naturally we got the mandatory photos and had their new CD signed, and after satisfying ourselves that *Holy Fuck* sounded about as bad as their name, we headed back to town on the tram. For supper we returned to Temple Bar for oysters at *Oliver StJohn Gogarty's*: yes, we know it is probably the most hyped tourist pub in Dublin, but we have always liked it and they serve the biggest and juiciest Galway Bay oysters you could imagine. Sated, we DARTed home and to bed. (We were greeted by a heron doing some night fishing on our pontoon.) By that night the increasing wind had reached over 30 knots, and Benj was up in his shorts at 0400, silencing frapping halyards, doubling up the lines and relocating fenders. Any thoughts of moving on the next day were quickly discarded! (We later learned that on that night in Holyhead boats had been blown off their berths, actually ripping the cleats from the pontoons, so maybe we were lucky to be as secure as we were.)

Sunday. More of a 'rest' day than we would have planned, waiting for the gale force winds to subside, so there's little to relate other than reading the Saturday newspapers, reading our books, eating and dozing: in other words just a normal Sunday chez Benjamins.

Day 20 Mon 4 June
Dun Laoghaire to Howth
Lat: 53:23.60N Lon: 6:04.00W

Having decided the day before that we would not be able to make the long passage north to *Ardglass* in NI because of the weather we awoke to a lovely sunny morning. In a classic error of judgement Benj thought we should just get off and go for it despite having missed the optimum tide. We stopped to refuel and were strongly advised by the man at the pump, an experienced local seaman who fishes for prawn on this coast, that we would not get very far against the ebbing near-Spring tide and that we should instead go as far as *Howth* and do the rest on the better tide the next day. What great advice that turned out to be! We did battle the tide to *Howth*, but only for 2hours, arriving in this lovely charming seaside/fishing harbour by lunchtime.

We berthed in the 300 berth marina and had a beer at *Howth Yacht Club*, one of the premiere clubs in Ireland, then did the tour of the town, market and harbour, and Benj gave the boat a scrub down while Cate hiked up to *Howth Village*, returning with more provisions. Unfortunately we then had to move berths twice in rapid and unprepared succession because we had been twice incorrectly allocated by the staff, in fact ending up where we had first stopped on our arrival. After a bit of sunbathing, we headed back into the main street for excellent fish and chips, which we cheekily sneaked onto the balcony of the Yacht Club and ate with our Guinness and Erdinger Alkohol-frei Wheat Bier! We repaired inside and had a good look round the beautiful club, with stylish modern furnishings and a large horseshoe-shaped bar, separate lounges and interesting pictures and trophies, some from major international events. Back aboard we watched a spectacular sunset over the harbour, looking out towards Ireland's Eye, a small unpopulated islet with a dramatic rock stack and Martello tower, which guards the harbour entrance.

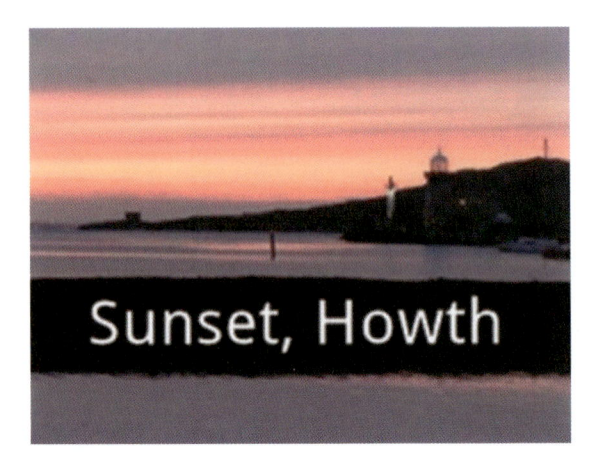

Sunset, Howth

Ninety-nine Days

Day 21 Tue 5 June
Howth to Ardglass
Lat: 54:15.63N Lon: 5:35.96W

This time we got the tide right, leaving at 0700. This was not long after Low Water Springs, and despite having done the calculations carefully, several times, it was with some trepidation that Benj (leaving Cate abed) set off down the tortuous and narrow channel out of *Howth* harbour, with less than a metre under the keel. Motoring past *Ireland's Eye* once again, we set course north, leaving the coast of Eire out of sight in mist and rain, aiming for *Ardglass*, back to UK soil. The tide was with us for five of the eight hours, but the wind strengthened again as we motored on using the radar to spot BFSs and the occasional other yacht. Had it been a clear day we should have had perfect views of the *Mountains of Mourne* (as they sweep down to the sea, tra-la), but instead Cate had to put up with Benj endlessly singing the song instead. Despite the heavy swell which gave us a Rock'n'Roll ride we fired up the oven and heated two Sicilian treats we had bought in Howth market - don't know what they are called[6,] but they are like miniature Vesuviuses filled with rice, meat, veg and mozarella - delicious hot food on the move. We made good time, but were nonetheless pleased to make it through the narrow gap into the tiny marina tucked into the corner of this fishing harbour. We were very glad of assistance from yachtsmen on the pontoon who took our lines (on Benj's second approach to the slot!). We

Rockbilly Light in poor visibility

---

[6] I now know they are called arancini, and we can get them at our local Sicilian restaurant in Deal

quickly put up the cockpit cover against the continuing rain, and changed out of one set of waterproofs into another and walked to the village.

There is essentially nothing in *Ardglass* apart from a shop and a pub, so of course we chose the latter. In fact the *Harbour View Inn* was a very friendly (albeit empty) place, taken over and refurbished two years ago as a family business, and we were looked after by Margaret, the wife, who told us there was freshly caught scampi on the menu. We decided to stay put rather than go back and forth to the boat in the rain and cold, so we did a bit of emailing (free WiFi there) and had early dinner (scampi and our first crisscross chips - very nice) with Guinness, then headed for shelter back on *Vega*. As I wrote this I had thawed out only by the use of our electric blower heater. The one thing I regret not doing in preparation for the trip is not having the *Eberspacher* heater replaced, but hey! £700 is a lorra money, so we just have to be good hairdy Scots and wrap up warm!

("Huh!" Cate reminds me. "It's OK for you 'hairdy Scots' but what about your poor freezing South African wife?". Oops, sorry again, darling.*)*

WEEK FOUR
June 6th – 12th
Ardglass to Ballycastle

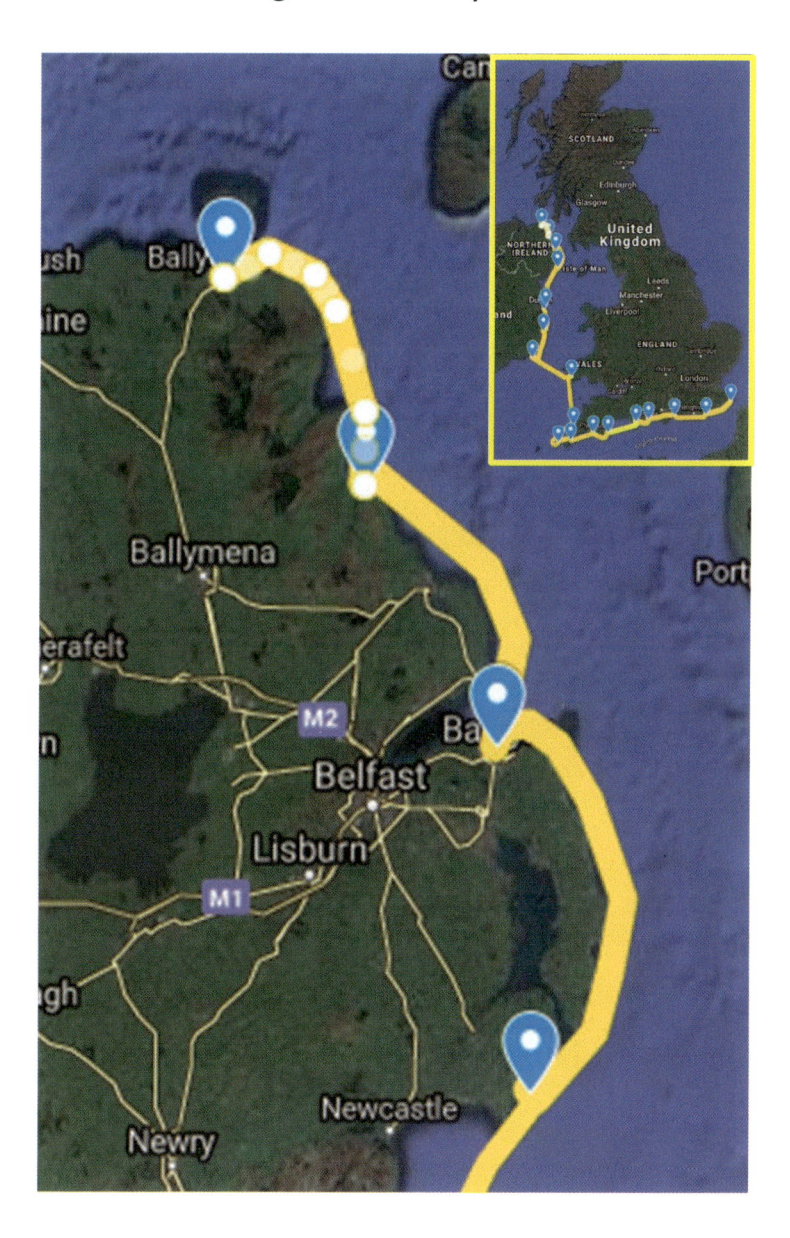

Cate and Irving Benjamin

Day 22 Wed 6 June
Ardglass to Bangor
Lat: 54:41.00N Lon: 5:40.00W

Because the north-going ebb tide begins at *Ardglass* at HW *Belfast* (1316) we were able to have a leisurely shower and walk into the village with a view to the All Day Irish Fry Breakfast at the *Harbour View Inn*. Unfortunately we found they had not yet opened at 1130, but we were met in the street by a friendly middle-aged local man who said his daughter would do us a good breakfast at the little shop further along the road, so off we went (in light drizzle!). Sure enough the daughter did indeed do hot food, though we would not have guessed that from the front of the shop, which sold everything from fresh fish to flowers to baby clothes, with bags of peat and jars of home made jam in between. The back of the shop was busy, but we found a table and had a superb breakfast with all the usual bad stuff plus fried soda scones and endless coffee refills. Stopping to buy some locally caught and preserved rollmops and a jar of blackcurrant preserve, we set off back to *Vega* and made ready to leave (remembering a day late to take down our Eire courtesy flag from the starboard spreaders – naughty!).

We left at 1250, and had a superb tide almost all the way to Belfast Lough, with zero wind, intermittent rain and some light fog patches. The route skirts a number of interesting rocks and lights, with names such as *Skulmartin, Burial Island, Butter Pladdy* and *Crooked Pladdy*. We also passed *South Rock*, which holds the first rock lighthouse to be built in Ireland, established in 1797, though now replaced by a light further out to sea. With the help of the invaluable Irish Cruising Club's pilotage book, we made our way through the passage between *Governor Rocks* off *Foreland Point* and *Deputy Reef* off *Copeland Island* on a mirror-like sea, a passage we would not have attempted in more hearty conditions, as the flood tide can rip through the overfalls at up to 4.5knots!

S Rock Light, 1797

Ninety-nine Days

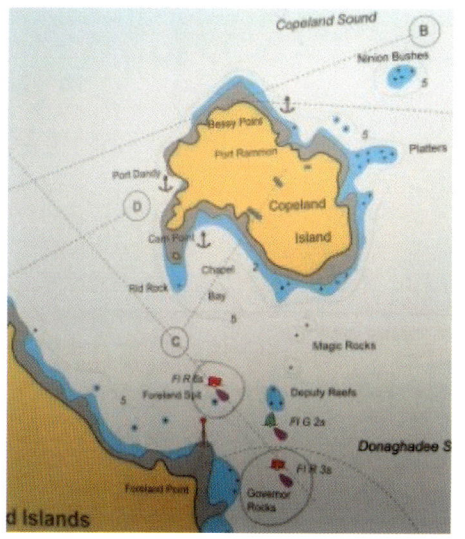

We tied up in the 300 Berth *Bangor* Marina at 1800, in time for Evening Prayers, with which we enjoyed our *Ardglass* rollmops, before doing a tour of the town. We were less than overwhelmed by what *Bangor* has to offer the visitor, and even struggled to find a pub we were inclined to patronise, and made the decision not to stay for an extra day, but to press on north on the 1300 tide tomorrow: little did we know then what the Met Office had in store for us! Read on.....!

Days 23-25 Thu-Sat 7-9 June
Bangor/Belfast … Gales Gales Gales (and rain)

It did not take long to work out that the Weather Gods were not going to be on our side for at least 48hrs. The whole of the British Isles was in the grip of strong to gale force winds, courtesy of a deep low moving slowly NE. We resigned ourselves to a stay here, and managed the first evening with a walk (a very wet walk) to the Omniplex Cinema, where we saw *Snow White and the Huntsman* (only in 2D sadly). Actually not a bad film overall, with spectacular effects and facial makeup changes, though such dialogue as there was is delivered in a very wooden manner, and the Huntsman's Scottish accent made Mel Gibson sound like Rab C Nesbitt! Takeaway pizza on the way home, and put the electric heater on again in the boat to dry/thaw out.

Retrieving my emails gave us a nice surprise in the shape of a new baby girl (Anya Chaudrey) to my nephew Anthony and his wife Sonia. Congratulations sent by e- and snail-mail.

We figured we had exhausted *Bangor*, so planned a trip into *Belfast* on the Friday, a 40 minute train ride along the shores of *Belfast Lough*, and found an historic pub - *The Crown* - with magnificent Victorian tiles, ceilings and wooden partitioned cubicles. A good lunch was had, supplemented for Benj with a couple of pints of *Coppertop* while Cate went off in search of the shops. Shopping proved a bit of a disappointment, being mostly big-name chains and characterless malls.

We met up again for coffee, and Benj set off in search of the Cathedral. It was hard to locate, made worse by the need for frequent sheltering from the intermittent torrents of rain, and when found it was firmly CLOSED!! My language was more suited to the outside of the church than inside, and after another drenching we made it back to Gt Victoria St Station. We mounted the train for *Bangor*, and Benj was immediately lost in the climax of his book (*At Risk*, by Stella Rimington, a good read) and Cate in her new Samsung Galaxy S3 phone. This had been the ill-famed joint belated birthday present, a pathetic attempt to make up for my miserable failure two weeks earlier in *Milford Haven*. As a result we failed to disembark at *Bangor*, the terminus! To our horror the train set off back towards *Belfast* at express speed, and we could do nothing but watch and await an opportunity to get off, which was at *Belfast* Central. The next train came along in less than 10 minutes fortunately, so tired and wet (did I mention it was raining?) we got home and cooked our shepherd's pie, with better hopes for the next day's weather.

Day 26 Sat June 9
Bangor to Glenarm
Lat: 54:58.00N **Lon:** 5:58.00W

Once again the tides rule on the coast of NI, so we planned to head north on the ebb of the *Belfast* HW of 1556. Cate did last minute wool shopping for the growing army of baby-knit recipients, while Benj readied the boat, and we slipped out of our *Bangor* berth to cross *Belfast Lough* at 1500. Thankfully we encountered very little commercial traffic (aka BFSs) leaving the docks, and we made between 7 and 8knots most of the way round *Black Rock* and past the high cliffs of *The Gobbins* (sic) where allegedly in the 17th century in reprisal for some crime, an entire village of 300 souls were cast over the edge.

The whole of this coastline is beset by severe overfalls (though not as severe as that suffered by the aforesaid villagers), and we bounced over some of these past the *Isle of Muck*, exacerbated by wind-over-tide conditions.

We berthed in the small, pretty harbour of *Glenarm* at 1900, greeted by the HM who waved us into a berth from the opposite harbour side. He then came down to greet us, plugged us in to an electricity point that did not need a card ("Not a very good salesman, am I?"), and took us up to see their brand new facilities, which are immaculate and well-found.

Glenarm is rather a dying village with signs that it was once a busy little community. There are 2.5 pubs (the 0.5 is the Barbican, which opens and closes 'every now and then'), two of which are tiny, side-by-side and almost identical. After supper aboard we did the mini-pub-crawl in company with the crew of *Juggler*, a Moody 38 who had been alongside us in both *Ardglass* and *Bangor*. Maureen and Brian hail from Derbyshire, keep their boat in *Pwhelli* in N Wales, and have been sailing up and down this coast for more than 20 years, as well as having done the Classic Malts Rally the year before us, in 2006. We enjoyed a pint of Guinness in each pub, and retired to our berth.

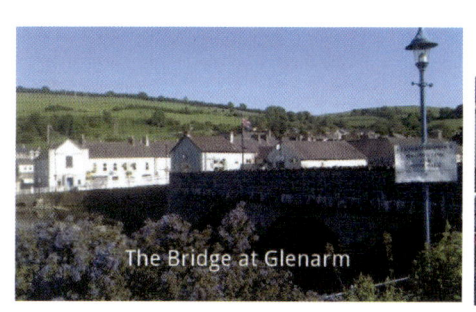

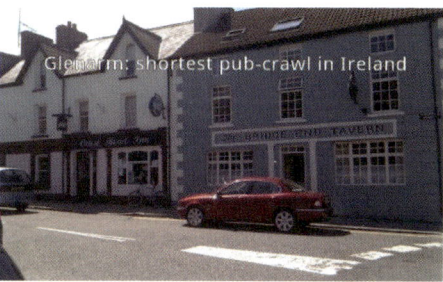

The Bridge at Glenarm

Glenarm: shortest pub-crawl in Ireland

Day 27 Mon 11 June
Glenarm to Ballycastle
Lat: 55:12.50 Lon: 6:14.30W

The Irish Cruising Club guide and Reed's Almanac are essential daily reading on this coast, as the on- and offshore tides are severe and sometimes unexpected. From *Glenarm* the north-going tide is again the ebb from *Belfast* HW, and if you miss that you are basically up the well-known creek without an implement. On this particular leg, rates of up to 4.5knots can be encountered, particularly around the headlands (*Torr Point* and *Fair Head*) and are accompanied by yet more severe overfalls, which you can only avoid by going several miles out into the North Channel, the policy adopted by *Juggler*, who were also travelling north today. We made a careful plan, and it worked like a charm, though if I were doing it again I would have gone about a mile further out to avoid what proved to be like the Rocky Road to Dublin at some points, with poor old *Vega* bouncing around like a bucking bronco. Leaving at 0630, we reached speeds of 10.5knots over the ground with the tide behind us, and were approaching the notorious *Rathlin Sound* by 0800. Inside the Sound the tide changes by the hour, swirling around every which way, all documented in the books, so you have to hit it just right, which we did, with only half a knot against us on the last mile of approach to the harbour. We couldn't raise the HM by VHF or by mobile (it turned out he had it on silent mode), so we crept into the small harbour and came alongside the hammerhead with a difficult side wind, and walked up to the marina office, where we were given the codes, shown the facilities, and directed to a permanent berth. The 74 berth Blue Flag Marina has been extensively upgraded. The office and facilities are all brand new, so much so that they haven't got round to putting in the coin slots for the laundry yet, so like good canny Scots we earmarked this to make use of the free wash before we leave!

Day 27 (Mon 11 June) cont:
Ballintoye Rope Bridge and Giant's Causeway

With the novelty of such an early arrival, we walked into the harbourside village (0.5 k walk from the actual 'town') and got lots of information from the very helpful tourist office, to plan our days out on the *Antrim* Coast. This was a stopover we had always planned for, with sights neither of us had experienced before. After much deliberation we opted for the local bus to *Ballintoye*, to do the *Rope Bridge*, with a Rambler ticket to get us to the *Giant's Causeway* and back. The plan was good, but marred in practice by the ordeal of enormously long waits between transports, starting immediately after 'doing' the *Rope Bridge*. It turned out that this was the only hour that doesn't have the Rambler bus, so we just lay on the grass and dozed in the warm sun until our transport arrived.

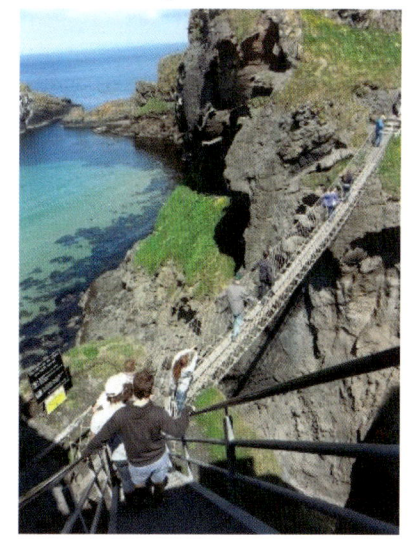

The *Rope Bridge* was made by the salmon fishermen in the 19th century, initially as a walkway with a single rope line, suspended across an 80ft gap between two rocky heads, in order to suspend their nets and catch the salmon as they run through the gap. It's now a major tourist attraction (National Trust, £5 a go), and there's a 1k walk down a narrow coastal path to reach the bridge (now with planks and handholds rather than a single rope) and cross the wobbling structure above the rocky water below to the 'island' where you can walk around and admire the views. Of course Cate, ever the adrenalin junkie, revelled in it, and Benj conquered his fear of heights by hyperventilating and not looking down despite jelly legs. Nevertheless a very worthwhile trip. Along the path, Jude, an entrepreneurial rather hippyish photographer, had set up his pickup truck and was selling his work, very good fine art prints mostly taken locally, and we bought a nice print of a dew-spangled spider's web, taken near *Torr Head*, around which we had sailed only that morning. As I write, I have no idea where that print is now: typical Benj filing.

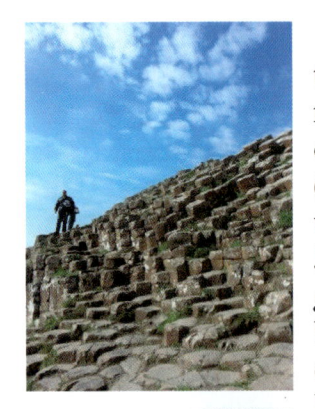

From the Rope experience the Rambler took us to the famous *Giant's Causeway*. There was a rather splendid-looking Visitor Centre (due to open next month), but for now it's another 1k walk (or £1 shuttle bus) down to the Causeway. We walked. It did not disappoint, considering that Dr Johnson had said *'It's worth seeing but not worth going to see'*- but then he didn't have the Rambler bus, did he? You are free to wander all over the extraordinary hexagonal stacks, and the site (a World Heritage site) is not spoiled by too many information posters etc, mostly just a few nicely made wooden block seats engraved with the images of what the rocks contain from the legend of *Finn McCool* - the giant boot, the organ pipes, the camel and the granny rock. We spent almost an hour climbing and walking around the site, taking photographs, and people-watching - there was a wonderful variety of shapes, sizes, ages and nationalities to see and enjoy.

We took the lazy (sensible) way and got the shuttle bus back up to the entrance, bought an informative book on the site, and caught our Rambler back to *Ballintoye*, and then the local bus home. The Rambler driver even stopped twice for us to get out and take a picture, or to point out some choughs which were nesting in the outlying rocky crags. (We are seriously *cr*p* twitchers, and have so far only identified puffins, shags/cormorants, shearwaters - though we don't know whether Manx or Great or what - herons, gannets, terns and now these rare choughs: when Benj did the east coast sail in 2008 with Clive Metcalf, Clive had pointed out innumerable different species, and we wished we could have had him with us on this trip.)

Ninety-nine Days

We had managed to skip breakfast and lunch apart from the odd snack, and were craving fish and chips, which we duly collected from *Morton's*, adjacent to the marina, and ate in the cockpit, enjoying the evening sun. The marina facilities include free WiFi and even a dedicated broadband network cable at a comfortable desk, so we both caught up with e-correspondence etc before retiring after 11pm. A super day encompassing an interesting sea passage, a trip to the village and two major bits of sightseeing. Glad we came to *Ballycastle*!

Day 28 Tue 12 June
Rained off in Ballycastle

We had been recommended a visit to the *Dark Hedges*, but rain and inappropriate bus timetables stopped play. Benj got the (very expensive) folding bike out for its first trip, but only as far as the Tourist Info Centre before the rain started again. There is only one very decrepit pub at the harbour in *Ballycastle*, so we couldn't even go for a Guinness. There is a rather fine hotel building - the *Marine* - but it's been closed for some time, an increasingly regular story round these somewhat depressed parts of *'Norn Iron'*, as they say here. So after a glorious sunset, more time to read, sing a few folks songs (also Benj's guitar's first outing for a very very long time), and sleep with the promise of better weather tomorrow.

WEEK FIVE

June 13th- 19th
Ballycastle (NI) to Oban (Scotland)

Day 29 Wed 13 June
Ballycastle

(In which our sailors venture inland to the Dark Hedges and get blisters on their feet, but no music)

The day dawned more promising, and we caught the 0945 Coleraine bus and were dropped off at the 'Dry Arch' as instructed, and set off along a country road to find this largely unvisited natural phenomenon. Beech trees 300 years old have grown together high above the narrow minor road in an unearthly tangle of branches and canopy. There is no sign leading to them, so you just have to know they are there, though there are plenty postcards in the tourist centre. Our walk there was almost an hour, plus the time spent taking photos. The experience of this magical place was well worth the effort. Walking though the long avenue of arches we could feel a supernatural calm and a numinous air of ancient mystery, and it was hard to tear ourselves away.

However, hunger and thirst got the better of us, and we navigated our way down further country roads (past a bear nailed to a tree, possibly a *'Deliverance'*-style warning the significance of which escaped us), eventually reaching the 'village' of *Mosside*, which according to the OS

Ninety-nine Days

The pub, Mosside

Good to know, esp here!

map held the promise of a post office and a pub. Surprise, surprise! This is north Antrim, and the pub hasn't opened for a long time, likewise the post office, and in fact all that's there is a garage, a tiny shop and the Orange Lodge Hall (with flags and bunting out for the Jubilee just past, including several from the Ulster Defence Force, now of course defunct, and various Red Hand banners). We were rather relieved to see the *'No Shooting'* sign nailed to a nearby tree. We were extremely lucky to reach the 'village' just in time to catch a bus at 1215, or we would have been sitting by the roadside for the next 2 hours!

Glad to escape *Mosside*, we arrived back in *Ballycastle* for a welcome Guinness (probably my last in Ireland) and a good bowl of seafood chowder at *O'Connor's Bar*, where there was to be traditional Irish music that evening, one of our reasons for staying the extra day here. However, we have long grown accustomed in our travels to *Benjamin's Law Of Pub Music*, which states that the music is always yesterday or tomorrow, but never today, and this was no exception! After a bit of provisioning and posh frock shopping we walked back to the harbour, sore-footed, and had afternoon tea and a nap before supper. Cate was looking forward to the plan for tomorrow: a short hop to *Rathlin Island* for the puffins, then a longer sail north to Islay, but even as I wrote this the forecast had changed, and it looked like we would only have a narrow weather window to get to Port Ellen on Islay before we'd have many more days of F7-8 winds, so it was off to bed for an early start. Yet again, Cate was frustrated and disappointed by the need always to have our plans governed by the weather, an ongoing theme throughout our travels.

Day 30 Thursday June 14th
Ballycastle to Port Ellen
Lat: 55:37.29N Lon: 6:12.26W

(In which our intrepid sailors brave the gales and make a safe haven in Scotland, only to be led astray by Irishmen).

Much debate on the harbourside with the crew of *Celtic Dancer* on whether to try to beat the impending gale or commit to at least a probable further 48 hours languishing in *Ballycastle*. The Met Office bulletin from 0300 was predicting gales in our waters 'later', which in Met-speak conventionally means 12 hours, so in theory we would be in *Port Ellen* before the storm hits. We all made the same decision - take the chance and at least be holed up somewhere different - so we skipped breakfast and *Vega* slipped out of the harbour at 0800 into the confused overfalls and cross-eddies of *Rathlin Sound*, with around 15knots of easterly wind. In view of the narrow time window we elected to motor, and we rounded the spectacular *Bull Point* to the west of *Rathlin* (Cate waving a sad, goodbye to the puffins) and set a course of 013° for 20 miles to Islay. The wind freshened as we went and the sea state (although in Met Office terms 'moderate') was what we would describe as 'lumpy' and very uncomfortable and difficult to steer all the way there. By the time we made the approach to the pontoons in *Port Ellen* there was a vicious cross-wind, and although there were plenty spaces on the fingers, we were predictably in some difficulty. Our predicament as we approached was spotted by other yachties, who clearly understood the problems, and stood by to take our lines. Benj made the first approach, but felt we were just too far off the pontoon for Cate to step off safely, and backed off quickly to circle round and try again. This was in retrospect a bad decision, as it would have been quite feasible for the waiting sailors to take our lines, and we would have been blown onto the finger. *(I have to record that this was pointed out to me later by Cate, who had actually been in a much better position to make that call than I. Not for the first or last time. Sorry, again, Cate.)* Two tight circles later and *Vega* was blown inexorably side on to two large fishing boats berthed alongside the harbour wall, and we had to rely on the combined brute force of both of us and three of the helping yachties to push us off enough to go round once more and make the final approach, doing it the way I should have done it the first time. We eventually were safely alongside and tied up with double warps in anticipation of the strengthening gale to come, and heaved sighs of relief: at least we were here, in Scotland even, and Benj celebrated that fact with a wee dram of *Old Pulteney* with our lunch aboard.

We went walkabout in the village (two hotels, two Spars, a tiny shop and what looked to us like a permanently closed pub, without even a handle on the doors) as far as the headland overlooking the bay, where the Cal-Mac Ro-Ro ferry was loading to depart. The road is lined with terraces of white-painted cottages, some in better repair than others, and we did a little provisioning at the Spar and took some pictures of the sun-drenched harbour, the calm before the storm. We both enjoyed a cuppa and an afternoon nap, and after Evening Prayers went in search of the *White Hart Inn*, which a sign told us offers showers for £3, including towel, as there are no actual facilities provided by the harbour/marina. In the lounge bar we met several crews, most of them watching Spain vs Ireland in the Euro football on TV. As we had our Guinness/tonic Spain scored twice making it 4-0, and a table of four N Irish sailors said it had all been going well until we arrived, for which we could only apologise! On our way we had met a sailor from our neighbouring boat, who said he was on his way to the 'whisky pub', which was the one we had believed to be defunct earlier. He assured us he had been in there until 0130 that morning, so it was very much alive and well. We walked on down there, and found the small bar and lounge buzzing with life, with much loud banter from locals and visitors, one of whom, showing little sign of consciousness, we watched slowly fall off his stool! The description of a 'whisky bar' was very apt, as there were scores of different malts on display, and a large printed folder of types and prices on the bar. Benj opted for a glass of *Kilchoman*, which was a new one on us, and indeed a very new brand altogether, distilled and bottled in a 'boutique' distillery on the island using all local produce, the first ever vintage being in 2004. The four sailors from *Skerries* who had been in the White Hart came in and we joined their table. Much banter and good 'craic', several drams and Guinnesses and a duet of *Rocky Road to Dublin* by Benj and their skipper later, we made our way home at 0130, having now missed dinner as we had missed breakfast. The gale was just arriving as we left, and the boat rocked and howled all night, and indeed all the next day, so we were very pleased to be tucked up safe and (almost) warm.

Ninety-nine Days

Day 31 Fri 15 June
Port Ellen
(In which the mariners remain stranded on Islay, make use of the showers, and watch football yet again)

After our late night we both slept until 10am. As predicted, the winds continued to batter the marina, and intermittent showers made even a walk or a bus trip uninviting prospects. Another good day for reading, knitting, the Daily Telegraph cryptic crossword (we did make it as far as the Spar to buy the paper), and a plan to visit the facilities of the *White Hart Hotel* for the shower and evening meal. We set off at 1930, and had good hot shower/bath and settled down by a large log fire in the hotel for our supper, while on TV England just edged ahead of Sweden (one token Swedish couple in the bar).

The meal was of mixed quality. My Hebridean Chicken, stuffed with haggis and black pudding, was excellent, but the scallops were under-flavoured and over-cooked, while Cate's langoustine tasted mostly of water. (Three rather dour Yorkshire sailors from *Emma Louise* shared our table. They were planning to leave for Oban on the next day and I don't think they believed my account of forecast 30k winds on WindGuru, but I noted as I wrote this the following day that they clearly thought better of it, as they were still here!) At the end of the evening we did eventually get a WiFi connection in the lounge by getting the hotel reception to reset their router, so we finished the evening with an email catch-up, resisted the lure of the whisky pub, and returned home to *Vega*, leaning into the F7 wind and slight rain, to a relatively early night.

Day 32 Sun 17 June
Port Ellen
(In which our storm-bound travellers try the island bus, experience fine seafood, and fail to experience Celtic Punk Rock.)

No significant change in the weather report, nor the wind and showers in *Port Ellen*. There is a bus which links all the small towns on the island, with a quirky timetable which differs from day to day through the week, to accommodate school days and non-school days, weekends and the daily ferry from Jura. We set out on the 1225 to *Bowmore*, with some previous knowledge, since in 2007 Cate, David and Mark Clough and Benj did the same trip and remember an excellent lunch at the only hotel, and visited the distillery (the only one of the seven on Islay that malts its own barley). The 20 minute journey is mostly a dead straight 8 mile road across peat bog with scattered sheep, passing the tiny airport. We headed straight to the Schooner Bar in the *Harbour Inn* for their pub food, and each ate six oysters from Loch Gruinart in the north of the island which were probably the best we had ever tasted, followed by a bowl of delicious seafood bouillabaisse with chunks of lobster and juicy mussels. The inside walls of the bar are decorated with coins stuck to the stone, a feature we had seen elsewhere, but for which the locals could give no good explanation: for luck maybe?

Cate explored the shops (there are about four if you don't count the Islay Whisky Shop) while Benj had another pint of 80/- ale and read his book. Benj bought a bottle of *Kilchoman* malt and one of *The Botanist* - the unique (and delicious) Islay gin flavoured with 22 local botanicals - then walked up the long straight hill which is the main street to the pretty white painted Round Kirk, built that way so the devil can't hide in any corners. We met up at the Co-op for essential provisions, and caught the 1550 bus back 'home' to *Port Ellen*. Benj returned to the White Hart to catch the second half of SA vs England rugby match, a thrilling half with the right result (Boks 37 England25). That evening there was music advertised in the village hall with *NiteWorks*, a band from *Skye* billed *as 'electric Celtic Rock'*. It wasn't due to start until 10pm, so we cooked a chilli con carne aboard and later made our way there, stopping at the 'whisky pub' for a last sample (*Caol Ila* was their Malt of the Month) and then moved on to the hall. However, because of the storms the band had not been able to get the ferry and had only arrived at 1030 and were just setting up. We went back to the White Hart and passed the time there and returned at intervals to check. By 1130 they were actually playing, but we took one listen and decided that the horrendous sounds of *Electronic Celtic Neo-Punk* were not our bag, and retired to bed. At least there was a promise of better weather for Sunday, so we retired happy.

The Round Kirk, Bowmore

Cate and Irving Benjamin

Day 33 Sun 17 June
Port Ellen to Scalsaig, Isle of Colonsay
Lat: 56:04.15N Lon: 6:11.00W

(In which we move to an even smaller island, taste even better oysters, and prepare to set off on an Adventure)

As promised the wind had abated and the sun shone, albeit weakly. We had planned a passage through the *Sound of Islay*, the narrow strait between *Islay* and *Jura*, in which the Spring tide can run up to 5knots, so timing was, as usual, important. We slipped our berth at 1000, and by 1230 had passed the distilleries of *Lagavulin* and *Bruichladdhie*, rounded Macarthur Head and were entering the Sound. The wind was still blowing 20k, absolutely on the nose, so motoring again, and the tide did indeed push us through at over 10k. We enjoyed spectacular views of the Paps of *Jura*, sunlit with a cap of cloud, and were passed by the CalMac ferry heading south. At 1400 we exited the Sound and headed out across open water towards , where the latest info says there is the possibility of berthing. As we rounded the breakwater of the Ro-Ro ferry berth it became clear that there is in fact berthing alongside the pier for one yacht, and it was occupied by a chartered Bavaria 47. The helpful crew of three couples helped us to tie up alongside, with long lines ashore to cope with the 2m rise and fall of tide, and we climbed the long, rusty metal ladder to the pier and walked past the (closed) ferry office to the (open until 8pm) *Pantry Tea Room* for quiche and my first Scotch Pie for several years.

Further exploration took us to the Colonsay Brewery, which was open, and we had a conducted tour, which took 5 minutes, of the small shed housing the equipment of the micro-brewery. The brewery is run by 10% of the working population of the island, i.e., two men. The barley and Kentish hops have to be imported, and the beer is now sent to *Alloa* on the mainland for bottling due to increased demand, apart from some kegs which provide draught beer to the only hotel on the island. We bought a few bottles and later sampled the draught - they make 3 varieties, an IPA, a dark ale, and a lager, all of which were excellent.

A notice in the *Pantry* window spoke of a knitter on the island who runs classes from beginners to advanced, and Cate left messages to make contact. *Yasmin*, the knitter, duly arrived to meet the 1800 arrival of the CalMac ferry from *Oban*, and called down to us aboard *Vega*. We were keen to do the walk to *Oronsay* next day (read on) and Yasmin offered to pick us up at 1400 at the Strand car park after the walk, bring me back to the boat, and take Cate to her home for an afternoon communing over knitting matters.

(We later encountered Yasmin's tups, which she had won in a game of poker, which sire the sheep she continues to raise on the island and harvest the unique wool, from which she makes her trademark *Gansey* sweaters. We also heard that Yasmin was recovering from a broken hip the result of being swung round by a fireman on her 40th birthday – they really know how to celebrate in the Hebrides!) The walk (it's coming, be patient, read on) is tide-dependent, so the only problem would be our neighbours in the Bavaria between us and the wall, who were leaving mid-morning the next day. Generously they offered that if we were not there they would do the complicated manoeuvre of slipping out, leaving crew ashore to man our lines, and tie us up again securely in our absence, an offer we accepted gratefully. That evening we walked up to the hotel and shared a dozen oysters yet again, this time even better than the Loch Gruinart ones, award winners for 'Best in Scotland' in 2009 and

2010, 'grown' and harvested by a Mr Abrahams of the island. Back to *Vega* for rhubarb pie and cream, and so to bed.

Day 34 Mon 18 June
Colonsay to Oronsay and back, on foot
(In which we see the sights of the island, and almost bite off more than we can chew, and Cate meets with her Hebridean knitting soul-mate.)

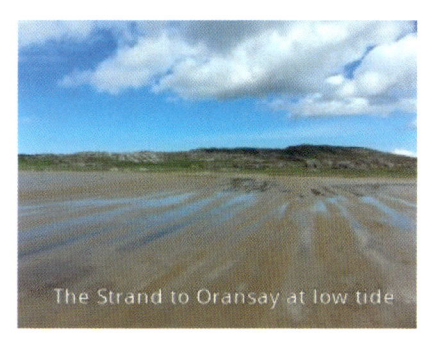

As planned, we set off at 1000 in wet-walking shoes and water and sausage rolls in our backpacks to catch the tidal window across to *Oronsay*, a small lump at the southernmost tip of *Colonsay,* only accessible across *The Strand*, a mile long sand flat, for 3 hours around low water - 1200 that day. Our first error occurred at about 1100, when we realised we had somehow missed the only junction on the track, and after stopping an RSPB van for directions we turned back to the correct road, adding an extra mile or more to the trip, and putting our tidal window at risk. The track now seemed endless, and much more up and down than we expected, but we eventually arrived at *The Strand* close to low water. *En route* we passed through the Valley of the Temple, where a tiny ruined chapel stands on a site where St Columba is said to have established a church before he went to Iona. We set off across the very wide open stretch of sand, not all of it fully dry (therefore wet feet) following footprints and car tracks. Once we reached the 'island' the track became very rough and our feet were already starting to suffer, and we were more than a little dismayed to be told by a returning 4-wheel drive that there was at least another hour to go to reach the Priory, the target of our pilgrimage. We pressed on nonetheless and when we did reach the site it proved well worth the journey (pacé Dr Johnson!). It is quite well preserved, with interesting cloisters and doorways, and a wonderful hall filled with gravestones and other monuments. It was in existence by 1353, perhaps founded by John of Islay, Lord of the Isles. It was dedicated to St. Columba, but very little is known about it because of the absence of records. The priory continued in operation until at least 1560, the year of the Scottish Reformation, with the last known prior, Robert Lamont, having been elected in 1555. The lands and property of the priory were given *'in commendam'* to Maol Choluim MacDubhthaich in 1561. T hey were later given to the Bishop of the Isles by King James VI of Scotland after his ascendancy to the throne in 1583.

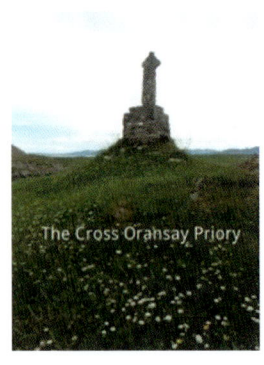

We only learned much of this later, and we could spend only a short time there before we were in danger of missing the crossing of the Strand because of the rising tide. We set off at a fast yomp, with increasingly sore feet and muscles, Cate almost in tears - it was less than six months since her bunion surgery! We did make the wet crossing (which seemed twice as wide as it had been going south) and were duly met by Yasmin, who dropped me at the harbour and took Cate home with a promise of hot tea, a comfy chair and an afternoon's knitting. Our boat had been re-secured by our kind departed neighbours, and I climbed down and scooped up a bucket of seawater over the side, and plunged my blistered feet into the icy liquid to anaesthetise them!

Neither of us had any energy left to go to the hotel, so we later ate aboard and took our weary but self-congratulatory bodies to bed early. Subsequent measurement on the chart showed we had walked over 14 miles, much of it rough going, so we did feel duly proud of the day's work. No need for an early departure next day, as the target was to be *Oban*, only 30 or so nM, with no significant tidal gate until *Kerrera* Sound, so we slept long and soundly.

Ninety-nine Days

Day 35 Tue 19 June
Colonsay to Oban (Kerrera)
Lat: 56:25.11N Lon: 5:29.84W

(In which we reach old familiar sailing territory and enjoy yet more fresh seafood)

We slipped our lines at 0800, just after the departure of the CalMac ferry. *(Cate pointedly asked me – "What? Eight o'clock start? Are we on holiday or something?")* Although we did have a brief trial of sail, the day really was a pleasant motor north-east between Jura and the Ross of Mull, and past the *Garvellachs* and *Seil Island* to enter *Kerrera Sound*. (Aside - we were sorry on this voyage to miss a trip to *Seil Island*, which we had visited in 2007. It is approached through a complicated rocky entrance to reach an anchorage at *Puilladhobhran* (pronounced *pulldoran*). Once at anchor we had dinghied ashore and walked over the hill to *Clachan*, where there is a feature known as the *Bridge over the Atlantic*, and a small inn, the *'Tigh-na-Truish*, transl - House of the Trousers. This is (allegedly) where highland men had to change from their kilts into trousers before crossing to mainland Scotland, the wearing of kilts having been banned by the English after the '45 Rebellion. And on our last visit we enjoyed delicious langoustine at the Inn, as well as purchasing some cards from the honesty shop next to the bridge. Ah well, can't do everything!)

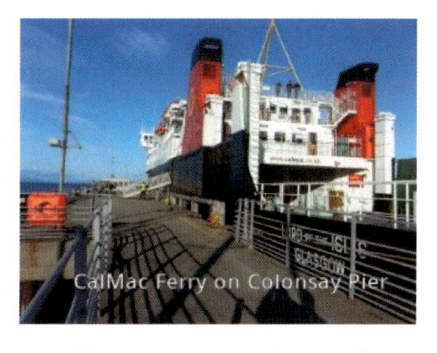

The passage to *Oban* was a mere 32 nM, and we were calling up *Oban* Marina by 1400 for a berth. The marina (which is actually on *Kerrera* Island, looking across the bay to the town of *Oban*), has expanded a lot since our last visit in 2007, and now has 130 pontoon berths (some for resident boats) and a number of moorings. We had some difficulty approaching a starboard-side-to 'closed' berth in a strong SE-ly wind, but tied up with some assistance from a neighbouring boat: I felt better when we had to render similar help to the next arrival!

We met marina manager Sue in the office and had a discussion about discounted berthing charges in view of our proposed long stay, and had our first meal at the *Waypoint Grill*. This used to be only an open marquee, but has now changed to a 'log cabin', providing much needed shelter from the elements, while still preserving the rustic charm of the place. (They did however make a Dutch sailor go out from under the roof and stand outside the open front of the cabin in the pouring rain, to comply with the smoking ban!) And the food was as good as ever, with excellent oysters (of course) and the knowledge that everything is locally caught and freshly landed. The seabass risotto was outstanding, and the cranachan for dessert is not to be missed!

Oban from Kerrera

WEEK SIX
20th – 26th June
Oban to Oban via Lochaline and Glasgow!

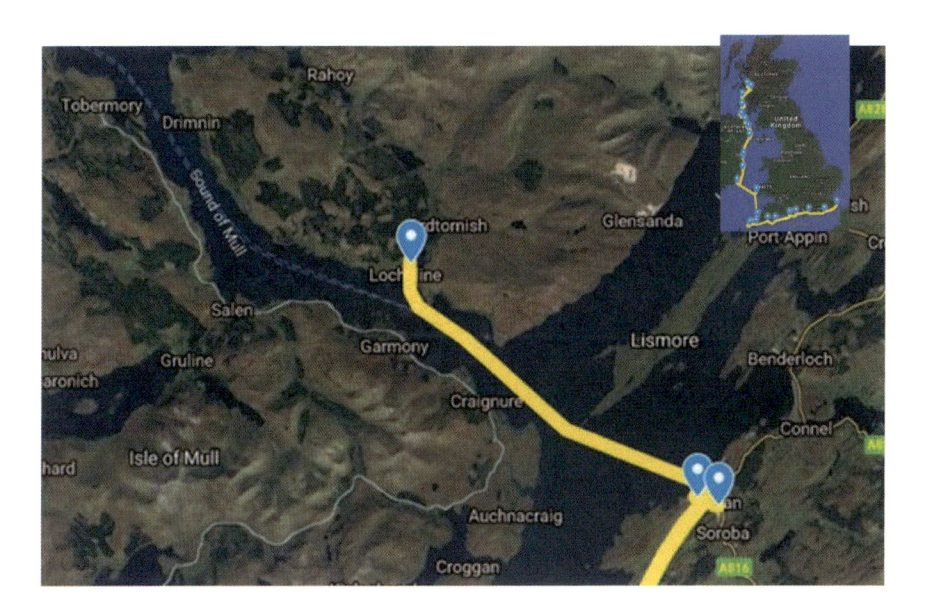

Day 36 Wed 20 June
Oban to Loch Aline
Lat: 56:32.60N Lon: 5:46.30W

(In which we meet Sandra Millar, puncture our bike(s) and greet Alek John Moroz into the world by WiFi)

Benj started by rising early and doing our first laundry for a while: there are three washers and two driers here, but you've got to be quick to claim one! Before leaving we refuelled, and then did slow circles round *Oban Bay*, re-aligning the compass on Otto, who worked much better thereafter. The plan for the day was *Loch Aline*, on the east side of the *Sound of Mull*. (We have learned this is pronounced al-INN, not al-INE. Locals get quite het-up about that!) On our 2007 trip to these parts we had made contact with Sandra Millar, an old friend of a friend of Cate's brother Hugh, and waved to each other and dipped our respective national flags as we sailed past her home on the hillside high above the loch. Since that trip the local authorities have laid pontoons on the loch side, and we planned this time to make a proper visit. The day was dull but dry, and with wind on the nose (of course) we motored out of Oban Bay, past *Maiden Island* which sits in the middle of the north-eastern entrance of the Sound of Kerrera, and headed for the Sound of Mull. The course took us past *Lismore Island* with its fine lighthouse, and the useful book Scottish Highlands and Islands suggests that the island has enough interest to be worth a future visit, probably by ferry from Oban with our bikes, to visit some ancient sites. [Retrospective note: we never did make it!] We also passed the splendid Duart Castle, standing high on a rocky outcrop on the tip of Mull, possibly also worth a later visit - if only we had more time here!

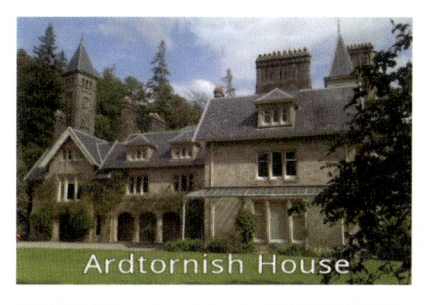

Onward to Loch Aline, where we found the brand new pontoons on the north bank, beyond the tiny village and ro-ro ferry pier and the jetty of the sand-works. This was built to service mines which produce some of the world's finest volcanic sand, valued for its properties for glass-making, but had fallen into disuse, making the establishment of the pontoons a valuable project for the economy of the area. However, the mines are now re-opened, and the noise of the workings rather detract from the idyllic nature of this beautiful secluded loch: such is progress! Sandra and her neighbour Neil came down to the pontoons to meet us, and we arranged to visit her later in the day. After a pleasant (apart from the noise of the neighbouring mining works) lunch aboard, we decided to erect our bikes for the first time and take the rough and muddy track to the head of the loch, and visit the gardens of *Ardtornish House*. Once found, we paid our £6 admission and spent an hour or so exploring the garden, which was laid out very much as a family home, a mixture of formal lawns and beds and quirky hidden corners and dense copses with rhododendrons and azaleas (just past their best). As we were making our way back to our bikes we were startled by a loud crashing from a dense wooded area just behind us, and a deer careered through the undergrowth and disappeared from Cate's brief view. We made use of the facilities and noted that there was game from the estate available from the freezers, and selected a pack of venison pieces for a casserole. The bike ride back seemed quicker than coming, though interrupted by Cate having a few goes on a rope swing along the track! Back at the boat we were greeted by the rather garrulous Pontoon Pete, who turned out to be a neighbour of Sandra's, and he extracted £19 for the night's stay. We then headed for the Dive Centre, which promised WiFi, as by now Cate was getting anxious for news of her daughter Noelle in Calgary, who was due to have her first baby (by Caesarian section) at about this time. After a welcome cup of tea at the Dive Centre - a very friendly casual facility for the diving community - we learned from Sandra that she has WiFi at home, and were invited to go there to await the news from Canada. It was then that Benj discovered a punctured back tyre, and with more than our rightful due of Highland hospitality, Sandra summoned Neil to come along to her cottage with his puncture repair kit, and we set to work in her kitchen (as it turned out with only temporary success!). In the meantime we both enjoyed Sandra's kind hospitality, Cate with tea and Benj with Chardonnay, and in due course the news came of the arrival of Alek John Moroz, Noelle and Jeff's first baby and Cate's first grandchild of her very own! Clearly an excuse for more wine for Benj, Neil and Sandra, and more tea and biscuits for Cate! Sandra presented Cate with a Loch Aline mug to commemorate the event. By the time we left I was on strict warning on my bike, having by Cate's calculation consumed two bottles of white wine (though Benj did feebly dispute the count), and we made it back to the boat safely and at least one of us slept soundly (and noisily as Cate reminded me).

Ninety-nine Days

Day 37 Thu 21 June
Back to Oban
Lat: 56:25.11N   **Lon:** 5:29.84W

Cate and Irving Benjamin

Day 38 Fri 22 June (B's Birthday)
Oban Town
Lat 56°24'55 N - Long 5°28'18 W

(In which the long-awaited [7]Delta Force Reunion, augmented by Cloughs and Bloxhams, commenced, and followed the customary pattern of hedonistic behaviour).

Packed for the weekend at the *Caledonian Hotel* (Cate only 6 dresses and 5 tops, with 4 pairs of shoes, Benj with completely inadequate waterproofs for the ghastly weather). The Oban Caledonian Hotel is most kindly described as 'tired' though there could be (and were) many harsher epithets applied over the weekend. However, the Dows were the first to arrive, and Susan had secured a table outside (the last time the weather would allow this for the whole weekend) and ordered tea for four. Benj met Iain at the bar and commuted part of the order into the excellent 'tea' made by the Belhaven Brewery, which set the pattern for the later arrivals. Willie and Laurie Fountain were next, and the Loudons (with the shortest journey to make, from Stirling) were predictably last. At about that point the heavens opened and we

---

[7] Delta Force, named after the Delta Club year of Glasgow Medical School graduates of 1970, is a group of four couples, all the men having been close buddies since the late 60s: Johnny and Jan Loudon, Iain and Susan Dow, and Willie and Laurie Fountain, plus the Benjies. DF meet once or twice a year for a few days away, sightseeing, eating, drinking, and exchanging the same old stories.

retreated to the hotel lounge.

With no prior plans for the evening, the boys went to recce the waterfront eateries, and made a reservation at *The Fish House*, where we reassembled at 1900, with wet umbrellas. The meal was excellent, with seafood of various species and cuisine styles, and well up to the standard expected for Delta Force reunions. We retired to the hotel bar, anticipating nightcaps (Gaelic coffee was a popular choice) to be informed that the coffee machine is shut down at 9pm, allegedly on orders from Head Office. Iain could not even get a Black Label whisky. There was a prolonged argument with the barmen, threats to write to management (Benj looked up the Mission Statement of the hotel group) and a bunch of very disgruntled DeltaForcers. Benj smuggled down from our room some tooth glasses and a bottle of *Glen Moray*, which had been his birthday present from Mel and Graham before we left, and the birthdays (including Birthday#1 for *Alek John Moroz* and *Thomas*, the new Fiona Dow/Bishop baby who arrived the same day) were duly toasted before we retired for the night.

Cate and Irving Benjamin

Day 39 Sat June 23
Wet in Oban with DF+4

(In which Delta Force are joined by Cloughs and Bloxhams, England draw with the Springboks in Port Elizabeth, and more good seafood is consumed)

The day was equally wet, and various plans were discussed over breakfast. Shopping, walking, and finding a sports bar for the rugby were all on the agenda. A sub-group set off to walk to Dunotter Castle, but turned back when the rain started in earnest, and about the same time Benj retreated on the ferry back to Kerrera to get some more adequate waterproofs, and Cate's non-alcoholic champagne for the evening. We reassembled for lunch at the *Lorne Bar*, some opting for haggis and black pudding, and others more sensibly a modest wrap in view of the meal booked for later that evening. Benj made a recce for the rugby venue, finally landing in *Coasters*, where he was joined by Willie and Iain, and then by David Clough, who had arrived in the meantime. He and Diane have been touring the Western Isles on David's Harley for the last 2 weeks, and this was to be their last weekend before heading south. David and Tricia Bloxham, doing the same tour by car, also arrived during the afternoon. The final Test in S Africa was a good game, and England can take credit for achieving a 14-14 draw (albeit not supported by any present in the pub). In the evening we all changed out of oilies and into our best frocks and headed to Ee-Usk for our 'posh' meal. Benj had a little contretemps with Mr Usk (?Mr Ee?) over the importing of Cate's pseudo-wine, but in the end he allowed its use on the basis that this was her very special occasion, probably helped by noting our table had just ordered 6 bottles of white wine just for the starter! The meal was, as expected, excellent (if pricey), and the craic was as good as ever with the Force. We had noted that there was a live band at the Lorne Bar, so we repaired there, listened to the 150dB sound at the open door, and decided a quieter pub would suit us better. The group, progressively diminishing in numbers, moved to *Aulay's Bar*, where a rowdy young crowd were in full flight, and ended the evening with appropriate nightcaps.

Ninety-nine Days

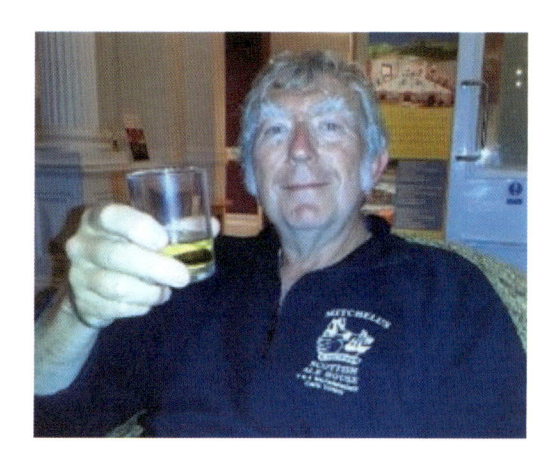

Day 40 Sun June 24
Oban - farewell to Delta Force

(In which we bid farewell to Cloughs and Bloxhams, introduce DF to the Isle of Kerrera, and forget to make the required time for the ferry back to Oban.)

We checked out of the *Caledonian*, making forceful complaints (along with several other residents) about the beds, the service, the rooms, the TVs etc. Apologies from the Duty Manager will almost certainly make no difference at all, but we resolved to follow up in writing to Head Office (for what good that will do). After photographs by the harbour wall and farewells to Bloxhams and Cloughs, we caught the 1210 ferry to Kerrera, where the meal did not disappoint the ever-discriminating gourmets of Delta Force! Those travelling onwards had set a deadline for the 1400 return ferry, which needless to say we failed to remember over our hearty lunch. So we all returned on the later 1500 boat, having made our plans for the next meeting (possibly Marrakech![8]), and had our farewell hugs and kisses. Another great DF weekend to go down in the annals. Back to real life, we bought a new travel bag for Cate from Argos, booked our seats for the rail journey to Glasgow, and back to *Vega* for Pot Noodles for supper!

---

[8] We did indeed go to Marrakech the following year, and had our usual great trip

Day 41, Mon June 25
Kerrera
(On which Cate spends the day packing, Benj keeping out of the way and doing light boat work and reading!)

Day 42 Tue June 26
Oban to Glasgow

On Tuesday the 1256 train to *Glasgow* was quite busy, so we were wise to have reserved seats. The rain wasn't too bad, so we could enjoy the views of *Lochs Tay, Awe, Lomond, Long* and *Gare*, and the long stretch along the Firth of Clyde through Helensburgh and Dumbarton to Glasgow Queen Street. The *Alexander Thomson Hotel* in Argyll St was too far to schlep Cate's bag in the pouring rain, so we jumped in a cab. The rain remained steady, not conducive to exploring the city, so we made a 100m dash to *Wetherspoon's* where Tuesday is Steak Night, and had supper there before an early night.

WEEK SEVEN
27th June – 10th July
Oban to Rum (via Glasgow)

Route of Classic Malts Cruise shown in RED

Ninety-nine Days

Day 43 Wed 27 June
Glasgow to Calgary or Oban
(In which Benj kisses Cate bye-bye, and visits an old mate)

The airport bus (one block behind the hotel) runs every 10-15 minutes and is good value at £5 single or £7 day return. Cate checked in at the Air Transat desk and we had a final coffee before it was time for her to go through the 'pinch', beyond which he could not pass (*sob*). So Benj returned to Glasgow, and contacted Bill Murray, former classmate from Medical School. Bill has had an unfortunate enough medical history both in himself and in his family, but it was capped earlier this year with a major haemorrhage which has left him in chronic renal failure, requiring thrice weekly haemodialysis. I had thought it a good plan to see him while he is having his treatment, for an uninterrupted catch-up. I could not for the life of me find the correct bus to the Western Infirmary, despite having been travelling on that bus almost daily for several years, and nobody in the street could enlighten me! So I succumbed and got a taxi, which did prove to have one nice side-effect. As we progressed westwards, I spotted the corner of St Vincent Crescent, where I had my first flat (just one room actually) away from home as a student. I got the driver to make a diversion, and stood outside my old tenement building and took a photograph: a man cleaning up the front of the building said I could enter and go upstairs if I wanted, but I declined and we carried on to the Western.

The dialysis unit is now in what was Sir Andrew Watt Kay's Surgical Unit, where I trained for one term as a student, and where Bill had worked as a House Officer and later Consultant, so it was very strange for both of us to be back in the old building. We chewed the fat for almost three hours, covering health, families (Bill's daughter Jennifer is being 'worked up' as a potential

24 St Vincent Crescent

live-related renal transplant[9] for her dad), music (he is still a very active guitarist with a rock band), medico-legal work, and travel. It was a good time together, and I was glad to have been able to do it. Sorry not to get to see Bill's lovely and devoted wife Isabel though: another time I hope. I left to catch the 1821 train back to Oban. It was a most amusing journey, as I shared the table bay with two very pretty gay boys, one of whom turned out to be a fashion photographer (he looked about 17) heading for a 'shoot' at a ballet school in Taynuilt of all places - who would have thought it?!

---

[9] She did donate her kidney, and Bill is doing very well to this day, without dialysis, as is his daughter.

Ninety-nine Days

Days 44-51 Thu June 28 - Thu July 5
(In which Benj passes the days in Oban in a mixture of Good Works and idleness, mostly in the rain)

Sunset over Mull

*"The Earth belongs to the Lord thy God
And all that it contains;
Except for Skye and the Western Isles
And they belong to MacBraynes"*
(*Anon*. With thanks to Dr Iain Dow)

Nobody truly wants to know what I did for this week, while awaiting the arrival of *Vega's* crew for the Classic Malts, so this is just the executive summary:

(i) *Useful things done*: (a) took bike to Nevis Cycles and got two new inner tubes, getting soaked in a massive thunderstorm in the process, bad enough that the passengers were refusing to get off the ferry from the marina to let us drowned rats on! (b) did a thorough clean and scrub of the outside areas of the boat, including the gelcoat still encrusted with the grit from Padstow; (c) installed new top guard wires - involving a rapid unscheduled trip to the chandler because Owen Sails had sent the wrong size clevis pins (don't ask); (d) serviced both winches (see pic - a first experience for me, with much trepidation), between showers, and on one side sheltering under an umbrella; (e) reorganise stowage on boat, including 'hiding' two folding bikes to make room for arriving crew; (f) constructed and replaced cockpit table toggle; (g) much Tesco shopping and re-provisioning.

(ii) *Nice things done*: (a) after much struggle and strife Cate and I managed to get electronic communications to work between us, including some late night/early morning Skype video calls on my magic Samsung Tablet; (b) walked to the Hutchison monument on the island to watch the sunset over Mull and moonrise over Oban (Hutchison was the fore-runner of the all-powerful Caledonian MacBrayne in establishing ferry transport between the islands); (c) visited the interesting St John's Episcopal Cathedral in town (it was extended but never completed); (d) watched Andy Murray's Fourth and Fifth Rounds at Wimbledon in *Aulay's Bar*, over a bowl of Cullen Skink and several pints of Guinness; (e) watched some good TV replays on iPlayer, while hiding from the rain, and read two good books; (f) supper of scallops at *Waypoint Grill*, and lunch of haddock and chips overlooking harbour wall (not on the same day!); (g) had great chat with Dave (Duffer) Neil, an Orcadian aboard *Capella Endeavour*, with useful information and advice about our plans for Orkney: believe it or not, this old salty dog actually lives in Ramsgate, and his delightful companion Jasmine runs a fish and chip shop in Broadstairs. Small world doesn't begin to cover it!

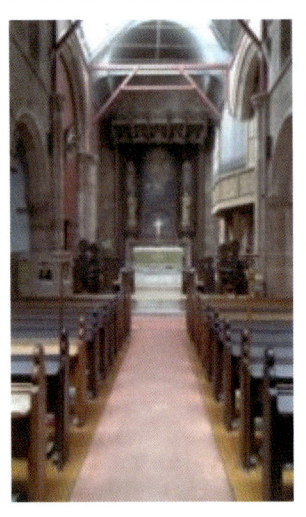

Well, that was it for the week, and as I wrote this (between blazing sun and sudden downpours), it was time to plan for tomorrow's arrivals - David Noble and Ian Sheldon - for the Classic Malts Rally. Watch this space!

Standard of Orkney

Day 52 Fri July 6
The Malts Crew assemble
(In which Benj begins the tale of his second experience of the World Cruising Club Classic Malts Rally)

Friday was the scheduled day for the Malts Team to assemble, David Noble and Ian Sheldon (aka Shelley) arriving by car from *Caster* (near Peterborough) that evening. I went to Tesco for final food supplies for the week to come, came home and cooked a beef and vegetable casserole in the pressure cooker. I got out the pre-strung signal flags (in the approved order, spelling no naughty words in any language, allegedly) and dressed *Vega* overall, including the 2012 Malts banner in addition to my 2007 ones, the South African flag for Cate, and the splendid flag with the ensigns of all the Celtic nations. I did one load of washing, as it was such a beautiful day, the sun shining brightly, and I hung the washing out to dry on the new guard rails, put my duvet to air over the boom, and settled down in the cockpit with my new book (a Michael Connolly) and my sunglasses, debating whether I should put sun screen on my legs or not: bliss! This is what it's supposed to like in July. Some 20 minutes later, as the first heavy drops hit me, I leapt up and retrieved everything, stuffing the duvet down the forward hatch, hanging the damp washing on the rails inside the cabin, and battening down the cockpit hatch. It stopped soon after, and I took the ferry back to Oban and headed for *Aulay's* Bar again (where I was now being recognised as a local) to watch Murray's Semi-final against Tsonga. Shelley had called earlier with an ETA of 1800, and called again at exactly that time to say they were unloading their bags on the North Pier. Murray was now two sets up, but Tsonga was coming back fighting in the third set, so I left my beer on the counter and hared off to fetch the boys to see the denouement! As any fool kno, Murray won in the fourth set, and we happily made our way back, unpacked David's car again, and ferried to the marina, where we had our Evening Prayers (introducing the crew to the outstanding quality of *The Botanist Gin* from *Bruichladdich*) followed by my equally outstanding beef casserole! David and I entertained ourselves (and as it turned out, our neighbours) with guitar, vocal and recorder renditions of folk and other songs, while Shelley kept his head down on his iPad, and eventually left us and went to his bunk! Surprisingly, no whisky was consumed that night, though I am sure that will be corrected in due course. Tomorrow is preparation day for the Malts.

Day 53 Sat July 7
Kerrera
(In which Benj shames the Maltsters by donning proper dress)

Shelley to the supermarket for essential supplies, most of which turned out to be cans of Guinness, John Smiths bitter and some red Leicester cheese! Benj to the post office to send Iain Dow's Senior Rail card back to him, but the post office was closed, so an entirely wasted journey, including long waits for the ferries. The free ferry service is what makes Kerrera a viable marina for Oban, and is reliable in as much as they run one or sometimes two ferries, on the hour, and will always return for more passengers if there are too many for one boat. For Elfin Safety reasons the boat can only take 12 passengers, so that there are often 20-30 people waiting for transport, entailing long waits at either end. The problem is that they now advertise the island's *Waypoint Grill* on the mainland as an excellent food venue, which it is, with flyers distributed around the town, so it is no longer just the resident mariners to be transported. Anyway, we made it back and still managed a smashing lunch at *Waypoint* in time for us all to get to a valuable Malts Skippers' briefing, about the route, the facilities at each venue, and the crucial tidal information about each passage.

We then retired to change for the evening buffet and ceilidh, Benj electing as usual to wear the kilt and, as it turned out, to be the ONLY one in traditional dress, with even the piper who welcomed us for our dram of Oban wearing jeans and T-shirt: poor show we thought!

Ninety-nine Days

The buffet supper was held in a large draughty boat shed, with the odd brave pigeon flying overhead, but the food was excellent, though the booze supplies were somewhat stingy. Initially in a light top, Benj was underdressed above the waist and had to go and change into a more sensible long-sleeved rugby shirt. The band (piper, rhythm and bass guitar and drum) led traditional Scots dancing, and there was much initial reluctance to participate, such that Benj, determined not to let the side down, had to kidnap a somewhat alarmed waitress for the *Gay Gòrdons*, having been turned down by the Norwegian ladies at our table. As things warmed up, he managed to join in the *Dashing White Sergeant* too, and by then the crowd loosened up enough (perhaps to do with the alcohol) to the point where they could even muster four sets for a *Strip the Willow*! Time for home, to prepare for the Parade round Oban Bay the next day.

Day 54 Sun July 8
Oban to Tobermory
Lat: 56:37.19N Lon: 6:03.87W

(In which David Noble pipes Vega round the Bay to start the rally)

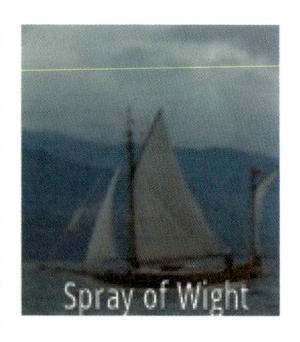

The first day of the actual Malts Rally began at 1045 with the Parade of Sail round Oban Bay, all boats dressed overall, led by *Spray of Wight*, a lovely replica ketch of the original *Spray* in which Joshua Slocum made the first solo circumnavigation of the world. On our previous Malts, *Spray* boasted a piper on her foredeck, but there was none this time. David Noble made up for this serious omission by standing on the foredeck of *Vega* playing an improvised 'Scots' lament on the descant recorder! The destination for the day was Tobermory, likely to be a hard 25 nM slog with both wind and tide against us from the north, but we duly hoisted the sails and did the best we could for a couple of hours, watching most of the rest of the boats disappearing into the distance (we are the smallest boat in the fleet), until we finally succumbed and motored in order to secure a berth. The harbour was already crowded as we arrived, and we felt sure we would spend the night afloat on a mooring, but we motored close in and David's eagle eye spotted the last pontoon berth, on which we gratefully tied up at 1700. We posed on the bow for the mandatory team photograph, and checked out the facilities. These are very new and pretty good, though the showers cost £2 rather than the usual £1, which caught a few people out who always carry their 'poon' in their pocket or wash-kit! The provided meal for the evening was fish and chips and a drink of your choice at *McGochan's* pub, but some initial false navigation led Benj and Shelley well past the venue and right to the end of the town. We made up for the error with a couple of beers on the way back at the famous *Mishnish* Hotel, and then returned for our fish suppers outside the pub. Back aboard another music session started, a bit louder and more confident than before, so Shelley went to bed and left David and Benj to their 'art'. An early start was planned for the next day, to catch the north-going tide around *Ardnamurchan Point*. A good end to a good start of our cruise.

Day 55, Mon July 10
Tobermory to Eigg
Lat: 56:54.50N Lon: 6:08.36W

(In which Vega rounds Ardnamurchan Point, winning the right to wear heather on her bowsprit)

This was the first day we have had to make a decision about our destination, as the fleet was not expected in Rum until the following day. The main choices were Loch Moidart, Muck or Eigg, and the committee decided the Isle of Eigg sounded the most interesting. After breakfast and our £2 showers we slipped the berth at 0900 and by 0915 we were under full sail, heading northeast up the Sound of Mull towards *Ardnamurchan* Point, one of the most prominent headlands in the West of Scotland, and actually the furthest westerly point on the mainland of the UK. We had calculated the tidal gate to give us the northbound stream round the Point, and the wind was forecast Force 3/4 occasionally 5, from the north. We put in some wide tacks to clear the Point, mostly in 15-18 knots of wind, sometimes inexplicably falling into a 'hole' with zero wind, only to pick up again slowly. Once round *Ardnamurchan* (which, incidentally, entitles us traditionally to place a sprig of heather on our bow) the wind freshened to a steady 20k, rising to 26-27. We took one reef in the Genoa, then one in the main, which made the boat much easier to handle, and were creaming along at up to 7k over the ground. The scenery was magnificent, with 360° panoramic views of mainland Scotland, Mull, Skye and the Small Isles (Canna, Muck and Rum) in pleasant bright weather. By mid-afternoon the wind had dropped to less than 20k, and David (who spent most time on the helm) suggested taking out the reefs. My customary practice when you consider doing that is to have a cup of tea first to make sure the decision is not over-hasty, so that's what we did (with cherry cake and cheese) and we then took out the reefs. Not too long after that, the wind freshened again and we were somewhat over-canvassed, but we soldiered (?sailored?) on until we were in sight of the anchorage at Eigg. This is in two parts, separated by a narrow channel leading to the ro-ro ferry pier, and one may anchor on either side of this. We motored slowly from end to end and selected a spot to drop our hook for the first time this trip, in a nice spot between the old slipway and the ferry pier, in 3m of water, making appropriate allowance for the calculated rise and fall of tide (though this is less than 3m in these waters). After some debate about whether or not to bother to dinghy ashore, the committee elected to go, and Shelley rowed us ashore in a stiff breeze, landing on a small beach below a steep rocky sea wall inside the ferry jetty. We walked to the 'tea room' which proved to be much more than expected: a tea room/provisioner/ island information centre and restaurant/bar serving a more than decent menu. Eigg is an interesting island, with less than 40 inhabitants, and no mains electricity. It had formerly been part of the Maclean family estates, but had been bought out by the 'natives' in 2007, and on each 12th June the residents celebrate their 'liberation' with an all-night ceilidh! It is a haven for wildlife of all kinds, and maintains an ecologically clean environment. We sat outside in the late afternoon sun with a stunning view, and enjoyed a sumptuous meal of mussels, smoked mackerel salad, and mixed Hebridean seafood, washed down with McEwans 80-Shilling ale (scrumpy for David), while watching other boats entering the anchorages. As we were finishing, Shelley spotted that our dinghy, which we had left high and dry on the beach, tied to the rocks, was now afloat in the risen tide, and he manfully strode back and retrieved it to a better position. We all walked back and this time David rowed us

back to *Vega*: both he and Shelley are experienced oarsmen as well as sailors, and are good at manoeuvring a rubber dinghy laden with 2.5 large bodies (David being rather petite in comparison with we other two), which is fortunate as Benj is a very unskilled rower! There was the prospect of live music at the 'tearoom' and David and Benj had seriously considered returning with their instruments, but thought better of it, faced with the prospect of a late-night row back against the wind, so we went to bed instead. A great day of sailing, and an enjoyable visit to a unique island.

Ninety-nine Days

Day 56 Tue July 10
Eigg to Rum
Lat: 57:00.56N **Lon:** 6:16.52W

(A glorious day, for once almost all spent under full sail)

We severally woke early and since there was no pressure of time on this day, went back to sleep, tired from the previous day's hearty sail, and all finally surfaced at 1000! The target for the day was the *Isle of Rum*, which as the Manx Shearwaters fly was only some 16nM away, straight into the northerly wind (forecast F3/4 occasionally 5, just like every day so far). A sensible plan was adopted, to set a long course east-ish towards *Mallaig* on the mainland, and then to tack back northwest-ish for *Rum*, both tacks being close reaches. This could not have worked better, and we had a wonderful day's sailing in pleasant weather and 14-20 knots of wind, making up to 7k over the ground. The tall mountainous shape of *Rum* grew closer and by 1600 we put in only our third *'Ready-About : Lee-Oh!'* of the day to approach the entrance to *Loch Snesort* on the island's east coast. As we approached, we could see more than 20 masts already at anchor in the loch. We had a serious struggle with the jammed Genoa furler (not for the first time in Vega's life: see entry on April 27, above!), some of which was only sorted after we had anchored. The reason is still unclear, as all had been working well until this time, but possibly related to movement of the spinnaker halyard while hoisting and lowering the ceremonial signal flags. *(Yawn! Sorry to any non-sailors for the meaningless detail!)* Once sorted, we headed for the Village Hall (by dinghy, carrying it part of the way over the slippery kelp foreshore to a better landing place) for a talk about the island. Some of us were rather sleepy during the talk, which covered the history, archaeology and wildlife of *Rum*, but finally by 1900 it was time for the BBQ, the fare including venison burger (and a plentiful supply of *Oban Bay* ale). We ate outside on the terrace, overlooking the boats in the anchorage, then headed back to the dinghy and thence to *Vega*, Benj rowing rather inexpertly with guidance from the others. It was apparent that our anchor had dragged, and Vega was heading slowly backwards towards the ferry jetty, presumably because of poor holding on a kelp bottom, of which we had been warned at the initial briefing. We re-started the engine, re-positioned the boat, and reset the anchor, with an alarm. A coffee and a couple of glasses of *Kilchoman* malt in the cockpit, admiring yet another spectacular Hebridean sunset, saw us off to bed, with the anchor alarm set on the GPS. At 0030 Benj heard the alarm and went outside to check, but all seemed well this time: a wide swing of the boat is enough to trigger the alarm, set to detect change of position of more than 0.01nM (about 60ft), so it is quite sensitive, but better safe than sorry. Later, Ian got up when the alarm went off, and reduced the distance to 120ft, and we were not disturbed again. More on the Isle of *Rum* tomorrow.

WEEK EIGHT
11th – 17th July
Rum to Inverie

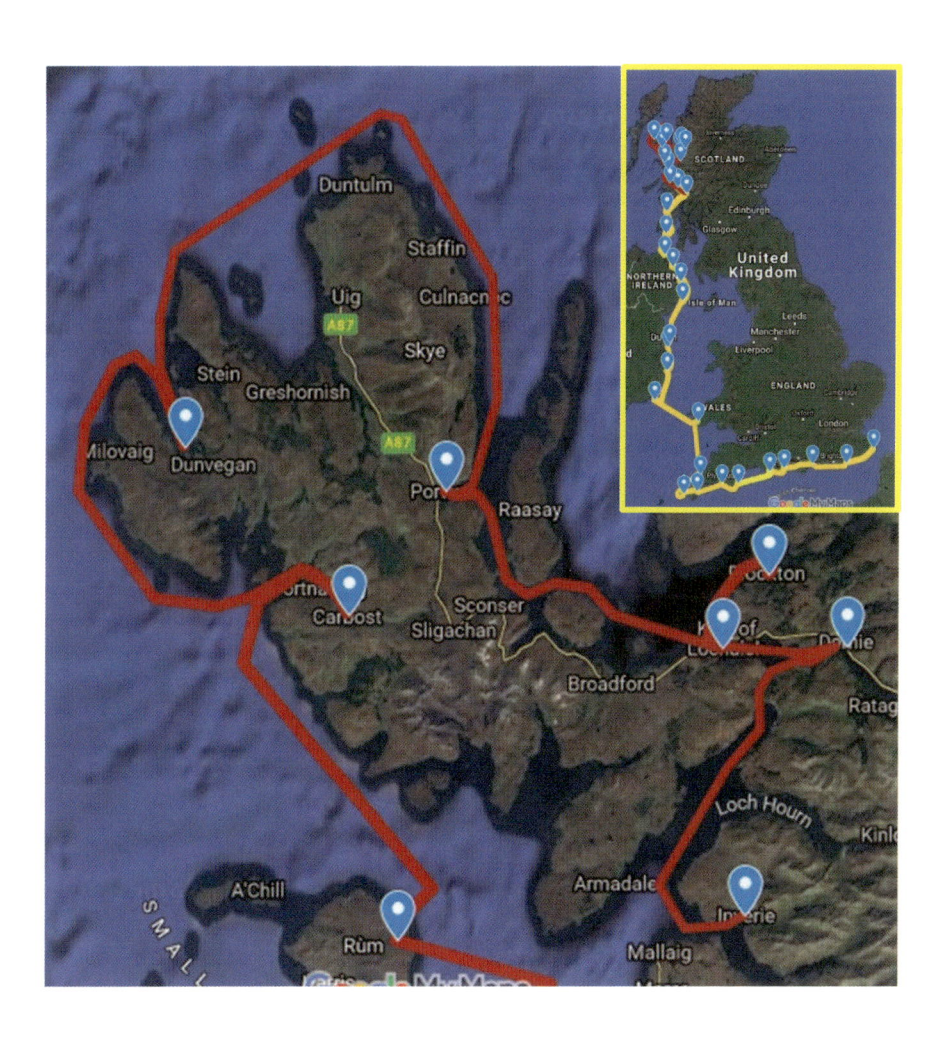

Day 57 Wed July 11
Isle of Rum
(A day of wildlife education and a unique stately home)

As we had booked for an eagle spotting walk at 0930 we had to be ashore in time to walk to Kinloch Castle for a prompt start. This time we used the outboard on the dinghy, which meant we could move more easily and further up the Loch to a large jetty, where we tied up and walked along the path, via a small, perfectly clean and useable, brick sh**-house. Our party of a dozen Malts sailors was met by our guide, a naturalist with Scottish Natural Heritage, who now own the island on trust, and we set off along the track up the glen to learn about and hopefully see some of the flora and fauna of the island. Rum had been part of the province of the Lords of the Isles, first Norse and then Celts, but following the Highland Clearances in the early 19th Century, the isle was owned by first by the Marquis of Salisbury and then by Sir John Bullough, a wealthy Lancastrian industrialist, who populated the island with deer and ran it as a private hunting estate. On his death the island passed to his son Edward, who set about building Kinloch Castle, a magnificent country house and estate with a commanding view down *Loch Snesort*. Shelley and I returned to tour the castle later (see below).

Our two hour walk was most rewarding. We did not see the rare sea eagles, but did see a golden eagle soaring over the mountain top, mobbed by a kestrel, the unique Rum ponies, and roe deer grazing further up the glen. The flora we saw included common spotted orchids and a rare Rum orchid, sundew insectivorous plants, bog asphadel, cotton grass and many others, too much for us to remember! We were mercifully spared midge bites, partly because we had each liberally applied our favourite repellent (*Avon Skin So Soft* for me, *Deet* for others) but mainly because the cold summer and brisk winds had kept the blighters at bay more than usual.

After a short stop for a drink at the village hall/shop/post office David went off to hire a bike to explore the island, and Shelley and Benj returned for a bacon buttie while awaiting the castle tour start at 1330. There were about a dozen on the tour, most having come for the day by ferry. The 'castle' - really more of a large baronial style country house - was built in the late 19th century as a huntin' shootin' and fishin' lodge, used for only a few weeks during The Season, but with a permanent staff of about a hundred. The large entrance hall is hung with more stag's heads than you could shake a big stick at, enormous stuffed fishes, portraits of the Bulloughs, including a fine one of Lady Monica. There are many stories about how Edward won his Baronetcy, including acting as a witness in divorce proceedings in order to save the reputation of the Prince of Wales.

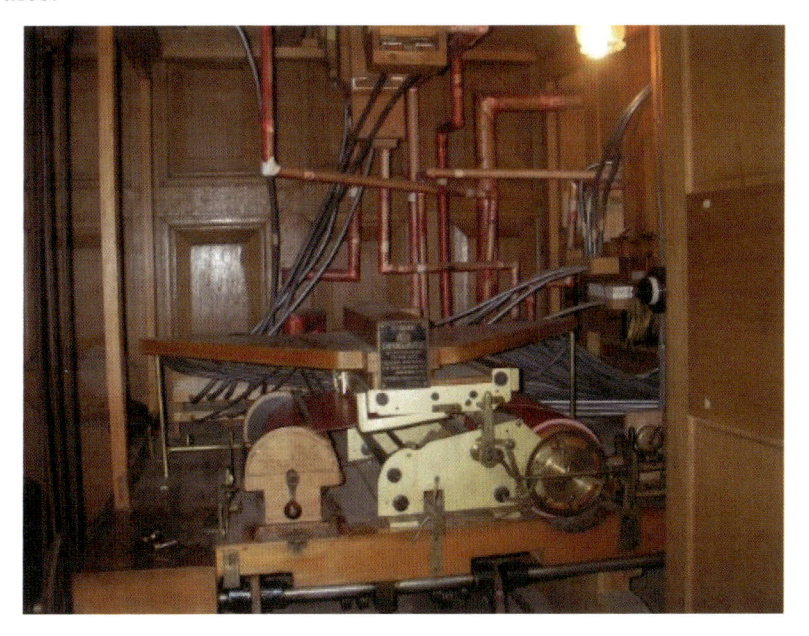

The room is dominated by an enormous bronze eagle attacking some monkeys, possibly a gift from the Emperor of Japan, and on the gallery two cloisonné work Chinese vases more than 6 feet high.

A unique feature is the Orchestrion, built in under the stairs. Our guide demonstrated the instrument, which incorporates a complete wind orchestra, with the addition of kettledrums, side-drums, tambourines and triangles. Like the smaller versions known as calliopes sometimes seen in travelling fairs, it is driven by perforated paper rolls, producing impressively loud music through numerous organ pipes, with an array of percussion effects. This is one of only two surviving models of its kind, built by Kaufmann of Dresden, a German family company, and the house has up to 40 rolls, though they have not all been tested since the refurbishment of the castle started. The tour continued through the bedchambers, some equipped with an en-suite bath/shower powered by an impressive array of tubes, taps, and shower heads designed to spray the user in all directions. The smoking room/billiard room has an early air conditioning/heating system, and this was the second home in Scotland (after Glasgow) to have electric lighting. The ballroom has (of course) a sprung wooden floor, a player piano and a minstrel's gallery. An interesting feature is the dining room, which has seating for 16, because the table and chairs came from the stateroom of Sir Edward's 261 ft Steam

Yacht *Rhuama*. Each chair has a hole in the centre of the base, which was fixed to the cabin sole when they were on board, so it could swivel to allow access. The yacht was loaned to the nation during the Boer War as a hospital ship and on display was a log of the patients' details, name, rank and condition treated: this is the 'official' explanation for how the industrialist gained his knighthood. The game record book was also displayed, showing that on some weeks one or more stags were stalked and shot every day, by gentlemen and ladies alike. Altogether a fascinating tour, and a glimpse of how the gentry lived less than 100 years ago.

    Shelley and Benj returned to the boat and later David hailed us from the shore, his ride to the further reaches of the island completed, some 26k uphill and down dale, in time for Evening Prayers followed by supper of pasta and red wine, and yet another spectacular Hebridean sunset.

Cate and Irving Benjamin

Day 58 Thu 12 July
Rum to Loch Harport
Lat: 57:27.04N Lon: 6:17.02W

(*'Speed bonny boat, like a bird on the wing, over the sea to Skye'*)

This was another slow start for most, though not for Shelley, who with great stealth took the dinghy quietly ashore early to shower. By the time the rest of us were up and about we had long missed the 0800 proposed start, though in truth the tides (now on Neaps) were pretty insignificant for our passage from Rum to Skye. Nonetheless this proved to be mostly a motorsailing day, with the continuing trend of F3-5 northeasters heading us. The weather was very pleasant and we had a relaxing passage round the east and north corner of Rum, with great views of *Canna* to the north west and the *Uists* on the far western horizon. The massive *Cuillins* of Skye loomed ever closer to the east, and of course we sang the obligatory *Skye Boat Song* until it became a serious brain worm.

We had predicted that as we turned round the headland into the entrance of *Loch Harport* we would be able to sail, and this proved satisfyingly true, with our last hour spent tacking round the dog-leg entrance to this spectacularly beautiful loch, heading towards the Cuillins. *Carbost*, home to the *Talisker* Distillery, the *Old Inn*, and not much else, came into sight, along with 20+ anchored or moored boats almost filling the bay. The next hour was spent trying to anchor, with several abortive attempts on deep kelp resulting in a dragging anchor laden with the dreaded weed. With most of the best anchoring spots already occupied by sailors who had got up earlier than us, the problem was that because the shores of the loch shelve very steeply, anchoring inshore in a useful 10m was all on slippery kelp, while moving only a few metres offshore placed us in enormously deep water. We eventually managed to anchor (securely we hoped) in water as deep as Vega's limit of 30metres of anchor chain would allow, and much anxious observation suggested we were steady and not dragging onto the lee shore. Shelley, by now clearly by default the Ship's Engineer, set to servicing the outboard engine, in which he had observed several defects the previous day. I, who had only ever cleaned the spark plug heretofore, assisted Ian as he dismantled the entire engine into more parts than I knew existed, and reassembled the beast just in time for us to motor ashore for the evening's entertainment.

After a beer in the *Old Inn* (and a shower for Benj), we were bussed via a very long road to the *Minginish* Village Hall, where we were greeted with a dram or two of 10 year old *Talisker*, followed by a meal of smoked mackerel pate, haggis with neeps and tatties, and sticky toffee pudding. The meal was all prepared by the catering staff of the Old Inn, but by a strange lapse of communication between the *Old Inn* and the *Talisker* distillery, there was no whisky available in the cash bar to anoint our haggis (which was, by the way, spicy and excellent). There was a talk and slide show by a local wildlife photographer, Jon Pear, with stunning illustrations of the local birds and mammals. (I did drop off to sleep, I'm ashamed to admit.) An interesting entertainment on the ride round the island was a varied selection of scarecrows, fabricated for a local competition. We all made our way home, eschewing a further visit to the *Old Inn*, and took the rather wet dinghy ride back to *Vega*. She seemed thankfully not to have moved in the meantime, and we shared a nightcap before retiring, the boat swinging wildly in the swirling wind up the Loch. We had viewed yet another gorgeous sunset, and as I wrote this log, at midnight, the western sky was still light.

Cate and Irving Benjamin

Day 59 Friday 13th (!) July
Loch Harport to Loch Dunvegan
Lat: 57:26.22N Lon: 6:35.19W

(In which the Malts crew enjoy the mandatory visit to what some would say is Scotland's finest distillery)

Vega was still in position at anchor when we arose this morning. We had booked for the 1015 tour of *Talisker* Distillery, so we downed our muesli and dinghied ashore in time. The tour was excellent, guided by a nice young lass who gave a very clear account of the workings of the distillery. Several interesting facts emerged, including that (like *Tobermory*) the recent dry weather (eat your hearts out you drenched southerners!) has meant that the water in the burn which is used to cool the distillate has dried up and slowed production to a low level. (It's not well known that it's the lack of water for cooling rather than for making the whisky that causes the loss of production.) The tour actually started rather than finished with a wee dram at 10am, which has given Shelley some ideas for the future! The tour ended with some purchases of the Wine of the Country, including the special edition *"57North"*, a blend which represents the latitude of the Distillery, the alcohol percentage of the vintage, and, er, the price! Shelley generously donated a bottle of this to *Vega* before we left: thank you Shelley!

We stopped at the *Old Inn* for coffees and our first reliable email and blog communication for some days, a welcome catch-up, and headed back to *Vega* in the dinghy.

Leaving Loch Harport

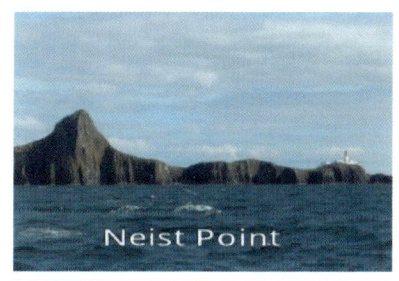

We finally sailed off our anchor (sailed, note!) at 1315, after all the rest of the fleet had left - last again. We sailed down *Loch Harport* and out to the *Little Minch* and round to the north along the northwest coast of Skye. We sailed on (reefed) in wind gusting to F6, passing some of the most spectacular scenery of western Scotland, with the west Skye cliffs soaring to over 300metres. As we passed the *Mibow Rocks, Neist Point* and approached *Dunvegan Head* we watched gannets make their dramatic dives, and elegant terns wheeling and skimming the water. Before *Dunvegan Head* the sea was distinctly bumpy and the wind was now on the nose, and for a time we motor-sailed. Just inside the Loch we were able to run down under Genoa, and after passing the splendid Dunvegan Castle, we found the anchorage at the head of the Loch with several Maltsters already here, and anchored with no difficulty. With the strong wind and the late hour making a run ashore unattractive, we dined aboard on chilli con carne. It seemed only fitting that we should start on our recent purchases, so we indulged in some *Caol Ila*, followed by a more or less improvised ceilidh, going through most of the Scots and Irish songs we know, Benj on guitar, David on recorder, and Shelley (reluctantly but effectively) on vocals, read straight from his iPad. A late and noisy night at 0100!

Cate and Irving Benjamin

July 14, 2012 9:40 AM
Digression: What's happening at home? Family news

While we lads have been exploring the Inner Hebrides, life has been going on for everyone else. Cate is still in Canada, having a wonderful time with new baby grandson Alek, mummy Noelle and daddy Jeff, and doing the Calgary Stampede and cycling the Rockies with son Keith. Comms have been difficult, but I have been able to receive a few pictures.

I have spoken a couple of times with my bairns. Daughter Lucy's house sale in Deal is all but through, and the Furnesses have been selling or packing all their goods for the migration to Perth (Oz, not Scotland). Grace (7) has just got straight As in her end of term school report, and my younger daughter Frankie tells me little Katie (6) has also had an excellent end of year report. I haven't managed to get a call to #1 son Matthew for a while, but I think he is in transit between Chile and Brazil as I write. I gather from Cate that all is OK with Leigh and Ale staying in our home at Taverners, though the house may soon become a bit crowded if the Furnesses also find themselves in need of a temporary home while they await their Big Day!

Anyway, we have now weighed anchor and are moving on in our Hebridean Adventure, so that's all for now.

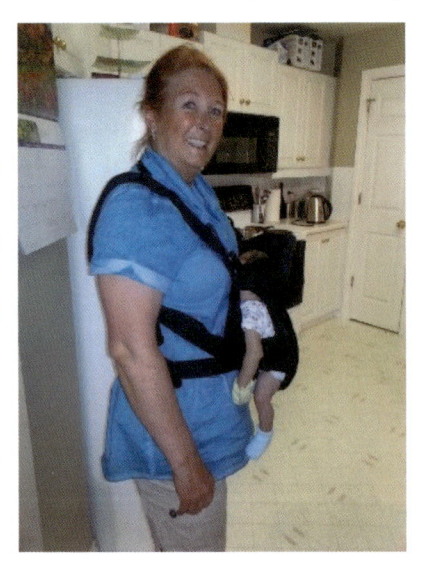

Day 60 Sat July 14
Loch Dunvegan to Portree, Skye
Lat: 57:24.45N Lon: 6:11.45W

(In which Vega reaches her furthest north point of the cruise so far.)

The Quaraing, Skye

Awoke to find Shelley already in the cockpit with the outboard in pieces and standing in a bucket (the engine, not Shelley), trying to adjust the running speed, which had continued to be hard to fix (in the end with still no clear result). We put the dinghy on the foredeck and were ready to leave by 1100, and sailed (again!) off the anchor. Our target was quite an ambitious one, depending on the wind and sea state, to sail right over the top of Skye to *Portree* on the east coast. The wind proved kind to us after we exited the Loch, with 16knots on the beam, and we were broad reaching at 6.8k for a time. We rounded the various rocks and islands lying off the north coast, and at 1400 we reached N58:43'.27 W006:22'.35, the most northerly point we will hit on the Malts Cruise, and the furthest north *Vega* has been. We sailed goose-winged for a time on a dead run east along the top of Skye, with *Spray of Wight* coming up behind us (not making up on us, mind) under full sail. She messaged on the VHF to say they were heading across to *Loch Torridan* on the mainland, but we did not change our plans in order to rendezvous with them for whisky nosings.

During the afternoon's sail we had wonderful views of the spectacular cliffs and mountains of the east coast of Skye. I recalled the land-based holiday Cate and I had previously enjoyed there, in particular the climb of the *Quaraing*, whose high Tolkien-esque peaks stood out against the clear sky, the mountain profile of the Old Man of Storr, and the impressive tartan patterns in the high basalt columns of the *Kilt Rocks*. Although the wind was usually a kindly 12-16k, this area is notorious for sudden and unpredictable downblasts from the cliffs, which on many occasions knocked the boat almost on her ear: one gust was measured at 32knots (F6), with an equally abrupt drop back to 12k, requiring constant vigilance from the helmsman. At around 1500 we were at last graced by a pod of dolphins, playing and leaping alongside the boat, until they tired of us and headed off to find another game. We made *Portree* at 1800, as usual to find a number of other Malts boats already on moorings, but we were lucky enough to find a vacant buoy and secured ourselves for the night without the effort and anxiety of lying to anchor in a strong wind. At Shelley's suggestion (prompted by yesterday's visit to *Talisker*) we changed our Evening Prayers routine by starting with a single glass of his donated fine malt whisky *(57N)* before our tastes were too jaded to enjoy it, which proved to be a good move. Our various information sources said we could get showers in one of the harbourside hotels, but when we dinghied ashore we found this was not so! We booked a meal in one of the seafood restaurants by the harbour and went to the bar of the *Pier Hotel* to drink away the interim. This was a very small bar, crammed with locals, most well-lathered by now and all very loud. The barmaid said this was the only pub in town, a statement we were to discover the next day was a downright lie, as there are several more salubrious-looking establishments up the hill from the seafront!

Nevertheless we enjoyed the craic and several pints, and then a meal of oysters from Sleat, scallops from Barra and langoustine from Mallaig, all delicious and fresh. Time to go home. It is a well-known fact that the most hazardous point of sailing is when three men travel back to their boat after a night at the pub in an unstable rubber dinghy. On this occasion the transfers were made OK, although a small error of navigation did lead to a gentle collision with a large, stationary, fishing trawler, much to the amusement of the young fisherman up on deck. (My lips are sealed as to who was 'driving' the dinghy at the time.) The rest of the motor back to *Vega* was uneventful, and Shelley and Benj had another glass of malt to round off a good day's sailing.

Portree Harbour

Day 61 Mon 15 July
Portree to Kyleakin
Lat: 57:16.39N Lon: 5:43.46W

(In which we sail under the Skye Bridge for the first (but not the last) time, and meet some friendly Dutch sailors)

Sailing south under Skye Bridge

Perhaps the final glass of malt was an error for Benj, as he woke up feeling distinctly under the weather this day, and later left even more of the work of sailing than usual to the boys. However, the first important issue of the day was to shower if possible, and Benj called the number for the *Harbour Lodge* B&B which allegedly offered this, but the owner, Sandra Campbell, said they stopped doing it some years ago. Nonetheless, having once been a sailor herself, she took pity on us and came specially to open up her empty self-catering accommodation to let us shower. She would not even take payment from us, which was beyond any normal hospitality even by Highland standards, and the shower was great and very welcome. Benj got provisions at the Co-op, and we sat on the harbour wall and ate haddock and chips from the chippy next door, first leaving a card and some chocolates for Sandra. We thus set sail rather late at 1400, after filling with water on the pontoon, and sailed down the Inner Sound between *Raasay* and Skye in a gentle wind, finally heading for the Skye Bridge. We sailed under the bridge with great views of the bridge itself, Skye to our starboard side, and a now disused Stephenson lighthouse on the island where Gavin Maxwell (of *'Ring of Bright Water'* fame) lived, heading for Kyleakin (pronounced kal-ak-in, emphasis on second syllable) hoping for a pontoon berth.

We found the small pontoon busy with fishing boats and a few yachts, but were hailed by the skipper of *The Moonshiner* to come alongside. This proved to be a rare treat, as *Sybren and Maaike* were kindred spirits, who had done the Malts Rally the previous year and were real characters. They at once invited us aboard for a whisky, of which Sybren is a serious connoisseur. They hail from Friesland in the Netherlands, where they founded and own a Scottish restaurant which boasts 400 whiskies! Sybren is a boatbuilder who designed and built *The Moonshiner*, a fabulous steel boat, the interior finished throughout in beautiful mahogany. They are full-time live-aboards. and the boat has a washing machine, water maker, full size shower, and two luxurious leather armchairs, and is altogether a craft of great beauty. The whisky on offer was no less - a single cask limited edition *Rosebank* (now defunct) and a rare *Talisker*, and there was whisky stored everywhere aboard the boat! Shelley (hereinafter to be referred to as McPhail, the engineer from the *Para Handy* tales) inspected the engine room, immediately spotted a problem, and offered to come back and help with servicing the next morning, which he did!

We made our way in a heavy downpour to *Saucy Mary's*, a combination pub/restaurant/shop/backpackers hostel, where we had an excellent meal (smoked salmon, chowder, chicken, pork and venison), washed down with a complimentary whisky because they got our order wrong. (*Saucy Mary* by the way was a Norwegian princess who tried to extract a toll for access to the Loch by putting a chain across its mouth, but was known for lifting up her skirts to passing sailors; well, I think I've got that right.) Back home, now in dry weather, but no music tonight, as we thought our Dutch neighbours were asleep.

Day 62 Mon 16 July
Kyleakin to Plockton
Lat: 57:20.25N Lon: 5:38.49W

[Digression: Monday morning, sitting in Kylerea now, waiting to move on to Plockton. Just received nice family pic from Cate in Calgary, and also news that Lucy et al have their proposed leaving date for Oz - 1st September! We had better get a move on if Cate and I are to get to Orkney and back in time for their leaving party!!!]

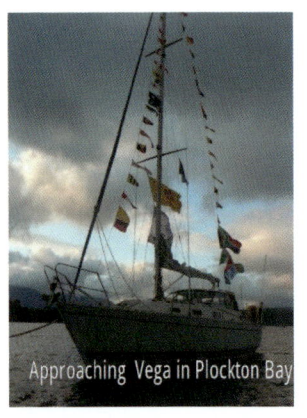

The day dawned with blue skies and HOT sun! We had our showers in *Saucy Mary's*, and Benj visited the Bright Water Visitor Centre, which has nice wildlife displays, particularly related to otters. Ian spent some time helping our Dutch neighbours with the engine of *The Moonshiner*, and we said our farewells and motored out, passing under the Skye bridge for the second time at 1145. The wind was a gentle SWesterly, and we ghosted along slowly under full sail, some of it goose-winged, and arrived in *Plockton* Bay at 1430. By now we had wised up to the fact that late arrivals don't get a mooring, so on this occasion we made sure we were there in time to get a nice (free) mooring buoy in the middle of the bay. *Plockton* is a very pretty village, like a smaller version of Tobermory, and was featured in the TV series *Hamish Macbeth*, and is a very active small boat sailing centre. We dressed the boat overall again, dinghied ashore and sank a couple of good Plockton Ales in the *Plockton Inn*, then returned to *Vega* to change for the evening's entertainments. This began at 1800 with whisky nosing and tasting. The *Talisker* team of young ladies had set out four tables on the lawn outside the front of the Inn, laden with tasting glasses of four different expressions of *Talisker*: 10-year old, 18-year old, Distillers' Edition, and , of course, *57North*. The idea was to savour one glass of each, but there was effectively no limit to how many each sailor could have. The crew of *Vega* were of course very abstemious (well, David was at least, but Shelley and Benj made up for him), and at 1900 we were prised away from the amber nectar to queue for the BBQ, which was hosted by the Plockton Small Boat Sailing Club, a very sociable group of sailors young and old, with a small but nicely set up bar/clubhouse. The venison burgers and sausages were washed down with a fine ale brewed in his microbrewery by club member Andy, who was also the fiddler in the excellent traditional Scots trio (fiddle, mandolin and guitar) who entertained us throughout the evening. Sated, we sang our way back to *Vega* for a relatively early night.

Day 63 Tue 17 July
Plockton to Inverie, Loch Nevis
Lat: 57:02.00N Lon: 5:41.20W

(In which we sail under the Skye Bridge for the third time, see a ghost, and carouse the night away.)

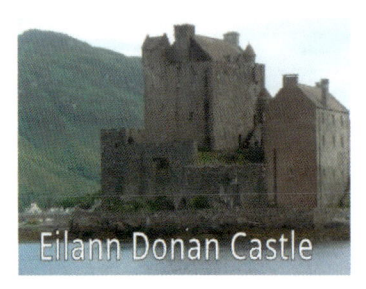

An early start this day because the tidal gate for passage south through *Kyle Rhea* is critical, since the flow can reach 6 knots on Springs. Our window would be between 0800 and 1130, and I was keen to fit in a wee diversion to have a view of *Eilann Donan Castle*, at the head of *Loch Alsh*, one of the most photographed sites in Scotland, popular for weddings despite the rumours of hauntings. We left at 0645, and there was just enough wind to sail under the Skye Bridge for the third time, with David a happy boy on the helm! (The trip has been regularly punctuated by differences of opinion between David, ever keen to sail, and Shelley, happiest when playing with motors or using his iPad! I was somewhere in the middle.) We sailed up *Loch Alsh* and had great views of the castle, including a viewing by David through his binoculars (he swears) of a Princess on the battlements. We thought he might have had too much Talisker last night, but he claims he has photographic evidence! Motoring back towards *Kylerhea* there were seals swimming around us. We entered the narrows in good time at 1000, and the tide progressively pushed us onwards, reaching 9.4k at the fastest part. The sea was very disturbed past the Kyle, with swirling mini-whirlpools all around us. We continued at a good rate, reaching *Loch Nevis* by midday, and entered *Inverie Bay*, where we easily picked up a good mooring by 1315. *Inverie* is a tiny community, consisting essentially of one street with a shop/post office and one Inn – the *Old Forge* – a famed traditional music venue. This is the most remote pub on the UK mainland, and is accessible only by boat, as we did, or by a 16 mile walk across hill tracks. The *Knoydart* peninsula in which it sits is regarded as one of the last great wildernesses in the UK, and is beloved of walkers and climbers as well as sailors. The area has no less than 4 or 6 Munros, depending who you believe. (For anyone who doesn't know, a Munro is a Scottish peak of over 3000metres, and Munro-bagging is a popular sport amongst hill walkers and climbers). *Knoydart* has an interesting history, celebrated in a plaque in the village. The land was owned by a rather unpleasant English landowner, Lord Brockett, and in 1948 a group of returning war veterans - the *Seven Men of Knoydart* - staked claims on the land, under an old Act of Parliament. They lost their case in the High Court, but in the end a community buy-out secured the crofters' right to the land in 1998. The events are celebrated in a song, which in fact Benj used to sing in his itinerant folk singing days with David and John Clough! You can find and listen to it online here:

http://www.youtube.com/watch?v=iXW_hSjxTo0

To this day the whole peninsula supports only around 70 people. We motored ashore and 'staked our claim' to a pint or two of the local ale in the *Old Forge* , and had a shower (£4, including towel!). Knowing the popularity of the place, we had taken the precaution of booking a table by phone that morning, and we later returned for dinner at 2000.

However, another treat awaited us first. Jeremy, one of the World Cruising Club organisers, invited us over for whisky nosing and tasting aboard *Spray of Wight*, including a good look around the boat, inside and out. (As I mentioned before, she is a replica of the *Spray* in which Joshua Slocum sailed solo round the world in 1898, and a beautiful traditional yawl she is, with all wood and brass and natural rope *fittings* and rigging). We were joined aboard Spray by a couple from *Nicole*, a

Jeannau 40 based in Glasgow, and two men from *Taurus*, an Irish boat. Jeremy guided us expertly through the subtleties of malt whisky tasting, sampling *Cragganmore*, *Dalwhinnie*, and *Bushmills* (strictly of course whiskey rather than whisky).

Returning to the *Old Forge* later we had a great meal, including fresh mackerel which we had earlier seen carried into the pub in a bucket, by the fisherman! The other thing for which the OF is noted is frequent spontaneous outbreaks of traditional music, helped by various instruments hanging from the walls. David and I actually took our own across in the dinghy, having in the interim even learned a local reel written in honour of the Robertsons, the owners, from a photographed copy of the sheet music on the wall! The ceilidh began after our meal, the two of us joined by another group, on borrowed *bhodhran*, guitar and tenor penny whistles, with some hearty vocals. The music went on until we were the last to leave at 0100, all sporting our new Old Forge T-shirts, bought for us by David. The dinghy ride back was, to say the least, interesting, partly because the boat was found left high and dry on the slip in the falling tide, and partly because we had not left a light on *Vega*, requiring some blind (?double-blind?) navigation. We made it safely of course!

Fresh Inverie mackerel

Ninety-nine Days

WEEK NINE
July 18th – 20th
Inverie to Oban

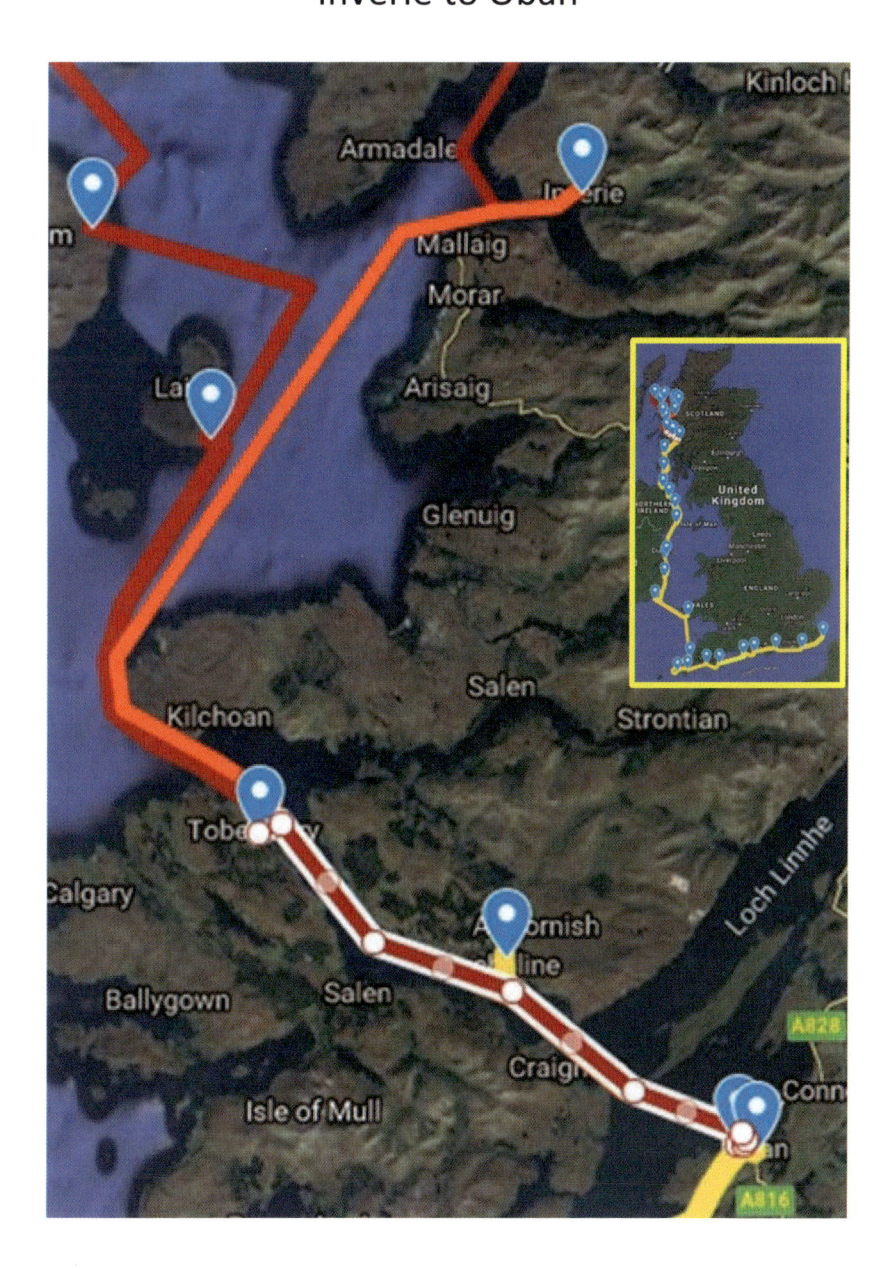

Day 64 Wed 18 July
Inverie to Tobermory
(In which we start our southward journey, and Noble stands guard)

We left *Loch Nevis* at 1000 under grey and drizzly sky with a light northerly wind, and headed back west for *Ardnamurchan Point*. This very dreich day was the first bad weather we had suffered for the whole Malts Cruise, good going for the West of Scotland. We passed *Mallaig* as the ferry was leaving, essentially motoring, albeit with a little assistance from the Genoa. We rounded the Point (do we get a second sprig of heather for that?) at 1500, and arrived in *Tobermory* Bay before 1700. Our plan was to refuel, and we gilled around waiting for a French boat to clear the fuel berth, while anxiously keeping an eye on (again) the last available pontoon berth, important as we were planning an early departure on Friday. When we got onto the fuel berth there was nobody serving, and Benj walked up to Mackay's Garage, who provide the diesel, to be told they finish work at 1700 (now past). Mr Mackay reluctantly said he would come down and fill us up, and while we were waiting we placed David on the vacant berth with orders to look his fiercest 5'6" and repel rival boats! By 1730 we were re-fuelled, safely tied up and ready for Evening Prayers. We showered and then ate at *McGochan's* Pub, where we met and shared a dram with Alexander Maclean, a delightful elderly local man who told us much about the *Mull* Highland Games which we were due to attend the next day: the Island and much else in the Inner Isles is Maclean territory, and the Games are referred to as the 'Maclean Games'. We were invited to visit him in the Clan tent tomorrow. Shelley and Benj had a walk along to the *Mishnish*, where there was a rather loud live rock band. It was the plan to retire early, but Shelley rather fancied the chance for a final session of malt tasting, so the two of us slipped into *McGochan's* again, where we sampled a few more drams of the 'wine of the country', before returning to find David already (wisely) abed!

Days 65-66   Thu/Fri July 19/20 –
Last day of the Malts, Tobermory/Oban
(In which we enjoy Highland Games, final tastings, and head for our last port on the Malts Rally)

Thankfully, in remarkable contrast to the day before, Thursday was gloriously hot and sunny all day. We set off in search of a cooked breakfast (remarkably, our first of the trip) and found *Tobermory* to be an almost breakfast-free zone! We were lucky to get a table at the *Tobermory Bakery*, which did a very fine Full Scottish Breakfast indeed. The parade from the clock tower for the start of the Games was scheduled for 1030, but actually set off at 1015, so we watched the Oban High School Pipe Band pass our window as we filled up with calories. We then walked up the long and very steep hill to the golf course, where the Games were under way. They had everything one associates with Highland Games: piping and highland dancing competitions, field and track events, and of course the so-called Heavy Events - throwing the stone, the hammer and tossing the caber. The event was very well attended, some walking round to watch the individual pipers being judged or visit the food and drinks tents, but very many families and individuals relaxed seated or lying comfortably in the heather on the hill which overlooks the arena as a natural amphitheatre, with views behind over the *Sound of Mull*.

We met Alexander Maclean again and signed the guest book in their Clan tent. Shelley and David left earlier than Benj; who stayed so as not to miss the caber tossing, but did get very hot lying out on the hill, and was pleased to get back for a refreshing bottle of cold ginger beer (no, really!) By 1800 it was time to change (second outing for Benj's kilt) and walk up to the Western Isles Hotel for the final meal of the Malts, preceded of course by a dram overlooking the bay. There was a flyover by an RAF Hercules, who dipped his wings as he passed, though there is considerable doubt that Andrew Bishop of the World Cruising Club arranged this, despite his claim!

The meal was a comprehensive seafood buffet, and we ate our fill, albeit for once mostly accompanied by water, as we planned to set sail for *Oban* that night. After the meal we said many farewells to our fellow sailors: there were some 28 boats with 90 persons on the cruise, including a dozen youngsters, from the UK, Ireland, Norway, Sweden, Finland, Iceland, Germany, Switzerland, USA and Australia, so there had been many tales to swop and experiences to compare. We walked back to the boat and prepared for our departure, as David and Shelley had to leave *Oban* early the next morning.

We slipped our berth at 1030pm, and headed south, motoring in the dying light. Benj took the helm (aided by Otto the Autohelm) all the way, which allowed the others to take turns to snatch a couple of hours sleep. The lit buoys and lighthouses along with *Vega's Simrad* radar and chartplotter make the night sail straightforward, and by 0230 we were seeing the lights of *Oban* town on the horizon. Once in *Oban Bay*, there was not enough light to find a pontoon berth in the packed marina, so we picked up a mooring at 0300 and retired for a few hours kip. At 0600, now full daylight, we cast off and hunted for a berth. Luckily we found a vacant slot on C pontoon, albeit one marked as Reserved. There was just time to unload and we all boarded the 0730 ferry to Oban. We said our farewells as David and Shelley loaded the car for their long drive down to Castor and Benj took the same ferry back to *Vega*, for some breakfast and to make a start on the laundry and boat cleaning, which would last this day and the next.

This has been a most successful and enjoyable Malts Cruise, in the finest waters of the UK, great sailing, good food and drink, and incomparable companionship: we all leave full of intentions to repeat the experience one way or another next year if possible.

For the record, here's a summary of how we spent the 2012 Classic Malts Cruise:

Nights aboard	13
Nautical miles	315
Hrs underway	65 (night hours 4)
Hrs under sail	36
Hrs engine use	37
Nights marina	4
Nights anchor	6
Nights mooring	2

WEEK TEN
24th-31st July
Oban to Portree via Largs

End of the Malts, and return of Cate to the cruise:
New line course in PINK

Days 70-74 Tue 24- Fri 27 July
Oban to Glasgow
(In which the Benjamin Team is reunited)

After some days of essential cleaning and washing, and a drink with Richard and Sue Calderwood, Dover sailing friends who now keep their boat *Sandpiper* in *Oban*, set off on the 1256 train from Oban to Glasgow. Checked into the Clyde Street Euro Hostel, nothing like as grim as it sounds, with a clean and adequate en suite room, albeit with bed springs which have seen better days. I had a pleasant evening diversion, to see *The Angel's Share* at the cinema: if you haven't seen it, you should do so, especially if you have any previous experience of Glasgow and its people. Next morning off to meet Cate on her flight from Canada, arriving 0900, then an overnight visit to John and Jill Clough in *Skelmorlie* (near *Largs*), including seeing John and David's 93-year old mum Irene[10]. We spent some time shopping in *Largs*, including a mandatory visit to this famous *Largs* store: note carefully the absolutely accurate wording on the sign! Train back from *Largs* to *Wemyss Bay*, on to Glasgow and the 1841 train to *Oban*, then picked up fish and chips en-route for the marina ferry, and that was the home team re-united and ready to continue our adventure. Friday was spent re-provisioning, and a very last meal at the *Waypoint Grill*, settling the bill for 26 days berthing (Sue and Maggs gave us a very generous discount), and checking the tides for the next day. Onwards and upwards!

---

[10] Irene Clough actually lived to celebrate her 100th birthday in 2019, surrounded by all her children, grandchildren, and great-grandchildren, and singing old music hall songs, but sadly died the following year.

Day 75 Sat 28 July
Oban to Tobermory
(In which we say our farewell to Oban/Kerrera and start the next leg of the circumnavigation.)

It was in grey, showery weather that we recommenced the cruise, leaving *Oban* at 0900 with a farewell to Maggs in the office. Wind was minimal, and inevitably on the nose, so we motored with a view to ensuring a pontoon berth in *Tobermory*, which we did at 1320. We were greeted on the pontoon by Richard and Sue Calderwood of *Sandpiper*, last seen in *Oban*, and their new crew. We did our laundry in the facilities block, but attempts to hang the washing out to dry on the rails in the pleasant afternoon sun had the effect of bringing on heavy showers of rain. We 'did' the town, showered later, and enjoyed some good pub grub in *McGochans* before retiring.

Ninety-nine Days

Day 76 Sunday 29th July
Tobermory to Inverie, again!
Lat: 57:02.00N **Lon:** 5:41.20W

(In which despite rain and midges, I introduce Cate to the delights of the Old Forge)

At 0830 I slipped the berth, leaving Cate to doze off her jet-lag, in heavy rain which looked set in for the day, heading for my final rounding of *Ardnamurchan Point* (are you sure I don't get extra sprigs of heather for that?). The wind was 12-18k from the NW, so once round the point I was able to sail for the next 4 hours under Genoa alone, making a steady 4-5+knots. The rain abated somewhat from time to time, but nonetheless by the time we picked up a visitors mooring in *Inverie* Bay it was in a fairly heavy downpour, and not conducive to a dinghy ride ashore. I had called ahead and booked a table for 2000 at the *Old Forge*, so we waited as long as possible before setting off for shore, in full oilies over our 'going out' clothes. We paused only for a photograph and got inside as quickly as possible to escape the midges, which this time had clearly not been deterred by the rain. The pub was already busy, with traditional music in full swing (fiddles, squeeze box and *bodhran*), and we stripped off the wet outer layers and found a table (and a pint of *Raven Ale*, and one of *Beck's Blue*). After a meal so generous we could hardly finish it (venison carpaccio, mussels, scallops) we sat back and enjoyed the craic. I could not resist joining in after a while, found the *Old Forge*'s guitar and sat in with the informal group, now expanded by a young woman

Music at the Old Forge

with guitar, a snare drummer with plenty enthusiasm but no sense of rhythm, a lady fiddler and two girls with ukuleles! While I was playing, Cate was fighting off the attention of drunken locals, and regularly replenishing my supply of *Raven* ale! The song and music went on until who knows when - we left at 0030. We had neglected to bring a torch, so had some difficulty finding our dinghy and getting safely aboard, but at least we had remembered to leave an anchor light (my new LED lantern) on *Vega*, so we knew where to go. The outboard started well, but stalled half way over, so it was fortunate that it was a dead calm night and easy to paddle the rest of the way home, the phosphorescence in the clear water sparkling round the paddles. We retired happy after another memorable *Old Forge* night.

Ninety-nine Days

Day 77 - Monday 30 July
Inverie to Plockton
Lat: 57:20.25N Lon: 5:38.49W

(In which Vega returns to Plockton, ducking under the Skye Bridge yet again)

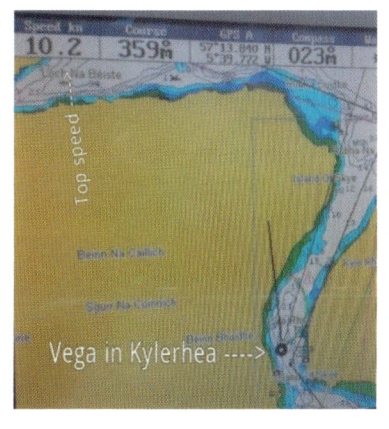

As we had discovered on the southward version of this passage the previous week, the essential feature of the plan is to hit the tidal race and whirlpools of *Kylerhea* narrows at the right time. High water at *Ullapool* was to be at 1753 BST, giving a tidal window of 1200 to 1600. We left rather early at 0830, in case of any unexpected holdup, which meant we were in the unusual position of having to slow down deliberately *en-route*. This proved a rather pleasant constraint, because it enabled us to put up the Genoa, turn off the engine, and ghost along gently at 2-3k for almost two hours, approaching the *Kyle* at 1230. The tide then quickly took charge, and we reached 10.2knots at the peak.

Once the *Vega* cork emerged from the Kyle bottle, the Skye Bridge came into view, and we motored again past the Stephenson lighthouse, undergoing renovation, and ducked under the Skye Bridge for my fourth time. Another hour or so brought us to *Plockton* Bay, where we picked up a nicely placed buoy and motored ashore in the dinghy for some provisions and a Hebridean cream tea (much the same as any other cream tea, since you ask) on the garden of the *Plockton Hotel*, watching the kayakers and dinghy sailors on the Bay. When we returned to *Vega*, they were about to start the evening club racing, and we enjoyed

Plockton

Club racing, Plockton

the mixed fleet of *Lasers*, *RS*s, *Wayfarers*, and local design boats as they tacked between the moored yachts, almost close enough for to reach out and touch, making us snap-happy with both camera and smartphone. We listened to the latest edition of *I'm Sorry I Haven't A Clue* on the radio, and cooked a supper of chicken tikka, followed by hot rhubarb pie with creme fraiche: we really *do* know how to live aboard *Vega*! We then enjoyed the constantly changing evening light, each taking far too many pictures yet again, and comparing the results on our respective devices for colour quality and composition. The final act of nature's show was a gentle sunset and a beautiful full moonrise behind the trees on the mountain top alongside us: Scotland at her best.

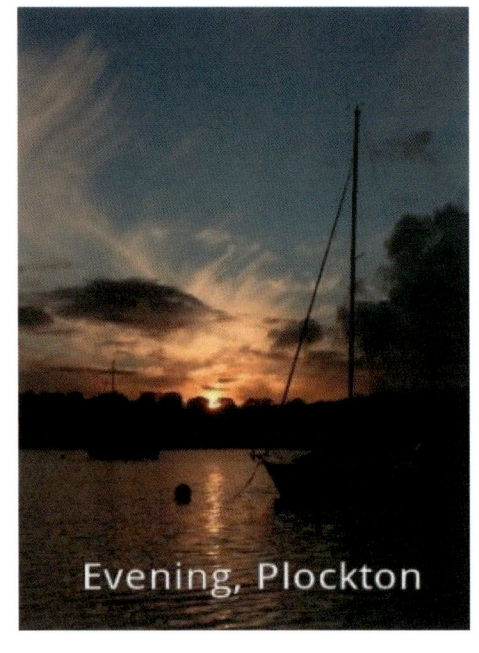

Evening, Plockton

Day 77 Tue 31 July
Plockton to Portree, Skye
Lat: 57:24.45N Lon: 6:11.45W

(In which we return to Portree and start to make plans for Orkney)

For once we awoke to blue skies and real warm sunshine, as if it was summer or something, so we cast off and headed (motoring, not a breath of wind) for the *Raasay Narrows* and the route north back to *Portree* on *Skye's* east coast. This was a short hop really, and we ate our rolls and growlers (pork pies for the uninitiated) *en-route*, and picked up a mooring in the bay at 1330. We had planned to land first on the pontoon to fill our water tank, but were waved off by the harbourmaster as there was a 600 berth cruise liner anchored here, and they had a constant shuttle of launches taking the passengers to and fro. When we rowed (see that? ROWED!) the dinghy ashore we found the small town was very busy with tourists of all nations, predominantly German. We had a coffee, and while Cate had some pharmacy business to deal with I had a beer sitting by the harbour, making sure our little rubber ducky did not disappear with the rising tide. As our holiday time is running short now, we have to make some serious progress northwards to have some time on *Orkney*, so we will need a few longer hops. One option for the next day was *Stornoway, Isle of Harris*, so I took some advice from the harbourmaster, and we looked at the weather together on his PC. Although we are due some nice steady light winds later this week, tomorrow will see ESE, with up to 25k, but some gusts of 36k, and he advised against *The Minch* in those conditions. So we will revert to Plan A, and aim for *Ullapool* tomorrow, leaving before 0600 to catch a nice few hours of northerly tides. Rowed home, cooked pasta for supper, and an early night for the early start.

WEEK ELEVEN
1st – 7th August
Portree to Wick via Orkney

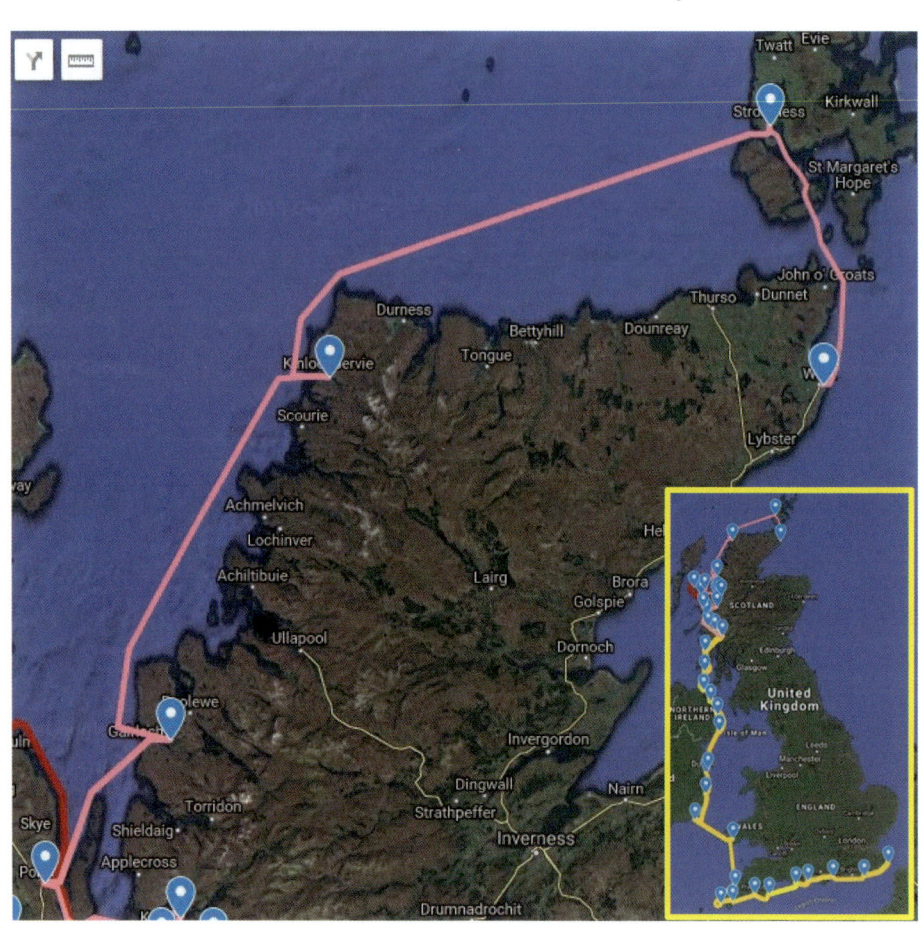

Day 78 Wed 1 Aug
Portree to Gairloch
Lat: 57:42.50N **Lon:** 5:41.00W

(in which we leave Skye, followed by dolphins)

Last view of Skye

dolphin off Skye

Predictably a difficult decision about the passage plan, with strong overnight winds and some long legs ahead, so Benj set the alarm for 0515 and popped out to inspect the elements. It was still blowing old boots, but the forecast was for the wind to drop away later. The prospect of another 24hrs on our mooring was not enticing, and nor was a trip ashore by dinghy, so we sat it out until an early lunch and cast off at 1230, motoring out into thick fog, with nav lights and radar on. As forecast, the wind had dropped to nothing, and the fog gradually cleared. As it did, we were greeted by an enormous pod of dolphins between *Skye* and *Raasay*, probably more than 30 in number, some of them leaping well clear of the water, frustrating any attempt to get good camera shots. We had to do some fiddling with the autohelm again, as Otto seemed to have developed some problem getting his compass heading right, but he did find his way, a great relief as we didn't relish the idea of hand steering under motor for hours at a time. We passed the impressive *Storr* on *Skye*, but the famous *Old Man* was mostly obscured by low cloud, with only what we believe to be his priapic organ poking out! As for the plan, it would now be too late to aim for *Ullapool*, so we opted for the shorter run to *Gairloch*, 27nM, and we entered the Loch at 1630. The current pilotage book said we might be able to get onto a pontoon, and even get showers and a shop, but by the time we arrived everything was just closed. (That included the little shop which holds the key to the showers in the sailing club - disappointing as we had now not showered for 4 days, and despite wet wipes we may have been getting a little 'ripe'!) The pontoon, tucked in behind the main jetty for the fishing boats, is quite small, and there was already a motor boat with a yacht rafted outside it, leaving just enough length on the near end for *Vega*. We came alongside, and were helped by the sailor from the yacht who took our line and assisted us to turn the boat round head to wind, which was brisk enough now to make manoeuvring tricky, and at 1710 I was reporting the end of our passage to *Stornoway* coastguard. We set off for *The Old Inn*, which gets good reports in the Highlands and Islands guide, had a couple of beers (the local brew, *Blind Piper*, for me) and followed the track to the *Flowerdale Falls*, half an hour's walk away, which were very pretty, and worth the effort. Back to the *Old Inn* for an excellent meal - stir-fried baby scallops in a piquant sauce, calamari with garlic mash, succulent venison steak, and a rich chocolate slice! (And a pint of *Corncrake*, an *Orkney* Ale, for me.) Back at the pontoon we filled up the water tank. We also put diesel from our 20L can into the fuel tank, as it is not possible to get fuel in *Gairloch*, even if anywhere was open, since the harbourmaster retired and has not been replaced. That lifted the fuel gauge to more than half full (capacity is 100L) which if necessary would give us enough motoring hours to get us even to *Orkney*, though we expect to be able to refuel before rounding *Cape Wrath* anyway. Early night again for a planned 0600 start next day.

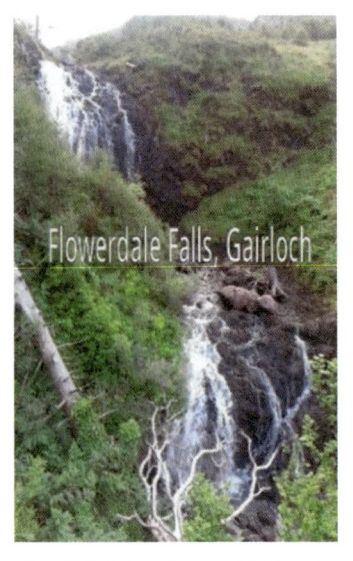

Day 79 Thu 2 Aug (Matthew's 40th birthday!)
Gairloch to Kinlochbervie
Lat: 58:27.26N **Lon:** 5:02.78W

(In which we refuel, and shower in a fish shed.)

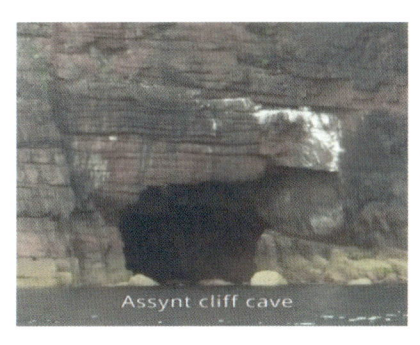

The planned early start worked better this time, casting off at 0545 into a lightening sky with a moon rising above a cloud bank. The weather forecast was pretty accurate, as we motored into 0k wind along the coast of *Assynt* and into *Sutherland*. Most of the time it was again *"Move along folks, there's nothing to see!"* However, the wildlife highlights, such as they were, included seals, basking shark (1), dolphins (1 large group), puffins (lots, but all on the water, and diving as soon as they see the camera), and lots of gannets. Interestingly their behaviour here is rather different from what we have seen before: they tended to skim the water and duck down for a shallow catch, as opposed to the more usual impressive Olympic-style dive from 50ft. (When you spend 10 hours motoring on a dead flat sea you have plenty time to ponder these matters.)

The scenic highlight of today was the impressive cliff formations, and in particular, passing close by the *Old Man of Stoer* to add to the OM of Storr on *Skye*: the next will be the famous *OM of Hoy*. (Why are these stacks all Old Men rather than Women? Maybe their vertical nature has something to do with it?). We had little more than odd showers during our long passage, but by Sod's Law, the heavens opened as we approached the near-invisible entrance to *Loch Inchard* for *Kinlochbervie*, our destination

We found the harbour at 1615, a passage of 10.5 hours, to find no space on the small boats pontoon, but rafted against a yacht from Brittany whose owners keep the boat over the winter in Scotland and sail here in the summer. We certainly needed to refuel, and established by shouts to a boy on a bike on the fish quay that they were busy and we should come back in 'a couple of hours' and tie up against the enormous rusty and weed-covered jetty. We headed instead to the harbour master's office, paid our £15, and went to the tiny shop for a few essentials. We then enjoyed our first shower for several days (see previous entry) in a Unisex facility with a single shower and no lock on the door in the fish shed (no kidding) - a first for both of us - and very welcome it was.

Unfortunately, we then had to return in the pouring rain to the boat, climb over our raft neighbours' foredeck, slip all our lines, adjust the fenders, motor 100metres to the aforementioned rusty pier, and tie up to get fuel, Cate skilfully catching and making fast to a long ladder. The dock worker dropped the long fuel line down to us and we refilled both tank and jerrycan. Benj then climbed the ladder, collected the docket, took it to the Chandlers (all still in *p***ing* rain), paid and came back, to find he had left the wheelhouse hatch open, so it was now full of water! Meanwhile Cate remained standing on the burning - correction *p***ing* - deck, fending us off the rusty ladder and finding her 'waterproofs' fell far short of the name. Cast off again and back alongside our French friends, and started to strip off our wet gear. Couldn't contact *Stornoway* Coastguard on VHF, and eventually found a land line number to report completion of our passage and get the next day's forecast (very light wind), and as I wrote this were tucked up cosy aboard with the promise of another early start, but a fine weekend in *Orkney* awaiting.

(Talking later with Cate about this in 2020, tucked up together warmly at home during the final weeks of her life, I can now better appreciate in retrospect her feelings about sailing, and admire the fortitude with which she tolerated and supported what was, in all honesty, my dream and not hers. Thanks for everything, darling Cate.)

Day 80 Fri 3 Aug
Kinlochbervie to Stromness, Orkney
Lat: 58:57.90N Lon: 3:17.70W

(In which we round the fearsome Cape Wrath, and enter the Orkney Isles in thick fog.)

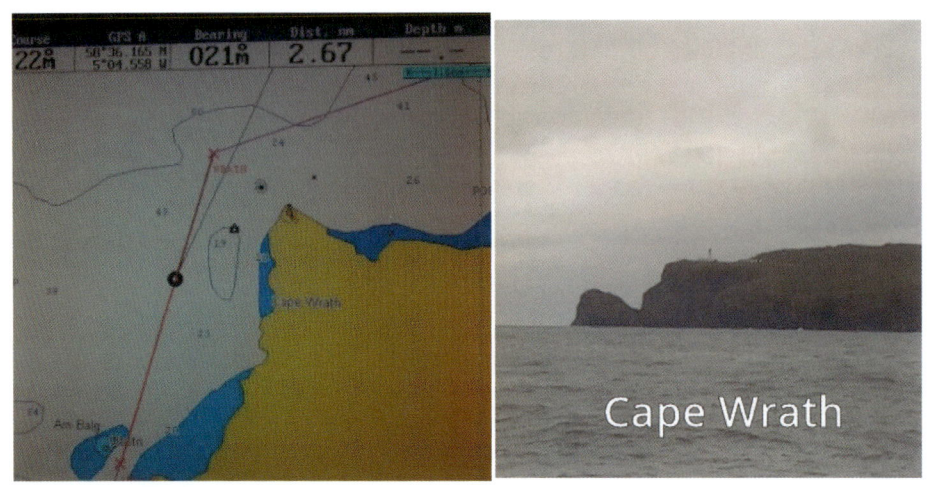

A pre-dawn departure (0515), timed according to the Clyde Cruising Club Pilotage book to hit the dreaded *Cape Wrath* at slack water, then pick up the E-going tide NE to the *Orkney* Isles, gradually leaving the Scottish coast behind. The day was grey and misty, turning to thicker and thicker fog as we progressed, and the wind was again nil, so we were pleased to have refuelled. We made good time, passed inshore of *Am Balg* rock, and rounded *Cape Wrath* at 0730, at a safe distance of 2nM. From there our course was a constant 075° making over 7k with the east-going tide. The radar had little news for us, only having to alter course once for a BFS heading towards the Cape. The surface of the sea was calm, but a high rolling swell increased gradually as we got further into open waters of the Firth. We were disappointed not to see any more marine life (still no whales!) but were entertained by the sight of several Great Skuas (known in Orkney as 'bonxies') dive-bombing gulls, presumably to steal their food.

We could only tell we were approaching land by the chartplotter, because the fog was so dense we never saw the *Old Man of Hoy* to add to our collection of OMs, nor indeed any land at all, until we were inside the start of the Sound of *Hoy*. At this point, the autopilot seemed to lose all control, and even the boat's heading did not make any sense, and Benj was sure we must have hit one of the local magnetic anomalies marked on the chart. After a couple of minutes of panic the penny slowly dropped: we were now simply being headed by one of the notorious *Orkney* tidal races, and were being pushed every which way by 6knots of adverse tide! We could now just pick out the headland at the entrance to *Stromness*, and gunned the engine hard to make the narrow passage inside at just over a knot. Once through, all was calm, and we relaxed and motored gently up past the fishing boats and ferry jetty to *Stromness* marina, a nearly new facility of some 60 excellent berths, with only half a dozen yachts and a number of small leisure fishing boats. We were on our pontoon by 1630, pleased to have made our first rounding of the fearsome *Cape Wrath* in such benign conditions, and looking forward to a few days exploring Orkney. We had a beer outside the *Ferry Inn*[11] on the harbourside, collected key fobs for re-entry into the locked marina, had a first wander round the town (more of that later), and ate fish and chips in the last of the evening sun on a bench outside the Ferry terminal. We were joined by a very wiry and hairy man who we learned was from Hastings, in the process of walking round every mile of the UK coast, eschewing lifts, and mostly avoiding roads. Cate wanted to ask him why he was punishing himself and what he had done to deserve it, but didn't, but we did not somehow feel inclined to offer him a bed on *Vega* for the night: we think he would probably have refused anyway. We settled back down aboard and watched a scary movie on the laptop, though it didn't scare Benj so much because he slept through most of it, after the dawn start.

---

[11] The Ferry Inn and Stromness Harbour were used a central location in my speculative fiction thriller 'Albastan', currently awaiting publication!

Days 81-83 Sat 4 - Mon 6 Aug :
Orkney Interlude
(Where we at last achieve one of Cate's most wanted travel objectives)

Saturday: Stromness.

After the treat of a cooked breakfast at *Julia's Cafe* we went our ways shopping and exploring the town. *Stromness* (on the bay of *Hamnavoe* in the local tongue) has a history as a village from the 17th Century, and developed as a shipping and trading centre during the 18th-19th. A principal employer was the *Hudson's Bay Trading Company*, both for whaling products and the fur trade, and most of the Company's workforce in Canada were Orcadians. The main street in Stromness runs parallel to the harbour front, and the houses are built with their gable ends facing the water, with narrow alleys between leading to individual small wharfs and piers, many of them still there and in private ownership. The long winding street, with wide paving slabs and cobblestones changes its name every few blocks, and there are numerous plaques on the walls celebrating famous earlier inhabitants. Login's Well provided water for many famed expeditions, including John Rae and Capt Cook. The poet and writer George Mackay Brown wrote and spent his last years there, as well as the less famous haggis hunter Walter Dalrymple. There are several interesting galleries and studios along the street, and we found some unique gifts. Cate had the interesting experience of witnessing a 'Blackening': this is a unique

Orcadian variation on the stag party, in which the groom to be is ambushed, driven round on an open lorry with much banging of tins, stripped naked and tarred and feathered! The more modern equivalent uses treacle rather than tar, but in the version Cate watched, the victim was fixed to a lamp post with many yards of clingwrap, then force-fed beer down a wide-bore tube and funnel by a large crowd of inebriated youths, all of them muddy and several of them bleeding: not a ceremony for the faint-hearted! Cate filmed some of it and later learned that if you get too close they are likely to throw treacle at you, so she may have had a lucky escape.[12]

We spent much of the day searching for a car to rent to go and visit the archaeological sites of the islands, with no success: every car in *Stromness* and *Kirkwall* was booked up until the end of the month, because of the summer season and the number of cruise liners arriving. Our only alternative was a conducted tour, and on the advice of the Information Centre we called and booked with *Orkney Uncovered* for the next day. As you will read, we could not have done better. In the evening we returned to the *Ferry Inn* for supper and watched one of Team GB's most remarkable days in the Olympics: we have of course seen hardly anything of the Games so far, but this Golden Day was worth waiting for!

---

[12] A 'Blackening' also features in 'Albastan'

Sunday: The Neolithic Heart of Orkney

We were met as arranged by *Kinlay Francis*, with his VW people carrier, in the drizzle! He had planned an itinerary which included most of the archaeology of the Mainland of *Orkney*, including booking ahead for us for the sites which required it. We drove north to *Skara Brae*, certainly the most famous and best preserved Neolithic settlement in the world. Since about 3000BC it lay buried under the dunes until the winter of 1850, when a severe storm hit Scotland, and stripped the earth from a large irregular knoll, or 'howe'. When the storm cleared, local villagers found in place of the howe an intact village, albeit without roofs, but the site was not seriously investigated until 1927. The village consists of a dozen small houses arranged closely together with easy communication between individual homes. The houses were built into mounds of pre-existing domestic waste known as 'middens', which may have provided both stability and insulation against Orkney's harsh winter climate. Each house consists of a large square room of about 400 sq ft with a hearth, dresser, and sleeping space. It would have required cooperation between settlements to move the massive stones to build the dwellings, but it was not thought at that time that there was any larger 'community' involvement beyond this, though more recent work has changed this view (see below). It seems likely that no more than fifty people lived in *Skara Brae* at any given time. It is not known why the settlement was abandoned. We wandered freely around the site, with Kinlay as our guide. Although his specialty is the military history of the Orkneys, such as the crucial wartime events in *Scapa Flow*, he is equally knowledgeable about the Stone Age, and was an excellent guide throughout the day.

Near to *Skara Brae* was *Skaill House*, a fine mansion with lots of interesting internal features, which we explored.

Cate had been keen to visit the *Woolshed*, an establishment near the village of *Evie*, which specializes in wool from the unique seaweed-eating sheep of *North Ronaldsay*. Kinlay did not know the place, and it would be necessary to call to arrange a visit as it was Sunday, so he called his wife Kirsty to get the details and make the call. This worked well and we were greeted by Rosie, who showed Cate her wares and her workshop, and we left laden with a large quantity of *Ronaldsay* wool, Cate grinning widely![13]

The next stop was *Maes Howe*, a tomb chamber buried deep within the large grassy mound (Howe). Our guide there was Amy, Kinlay's cousin. We entered at a crouch through a 10metre tunnel, into the main chamber with deep recesses to three sides, which are thought to be where the bones of the Stone Age men were interred, though strangely only a part of each body, so that the bodies must have been de-fleshed somewhere else first. The mound itself is about 35m in diameter and some 7m high, and is surrounded by a wide circular ditch, all dated to around 3500BC. The tomb had been broken into through the roof by Norse invaders in the 12th century, and there are rich runic inscriptions on the stone walls. It was constructed so that the rising sun at the winter solstice shines up the long entrance tunnel to direct its light on the back wall of the inner chamber.

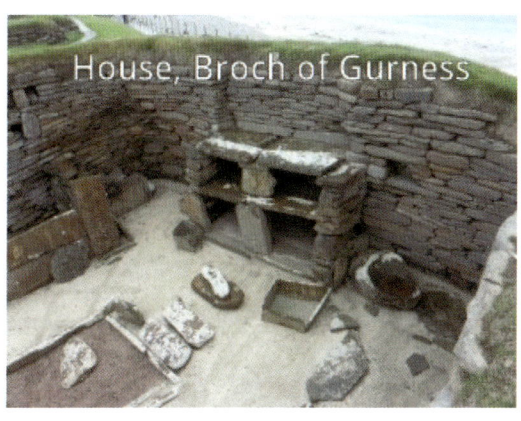

---

[13] Cate has since knitted traditional fishermen's watch caps in the unique wool, with her trademark 'Knitwit', which were sold in one of Deal's specialty shops.

We next visited the *Broch of Gurness*, an even more extraordinary settlement in a remarkable state of preservation. The remains of the broch were discovered by Orcadian poet and antiquarian, Robert Rendall. While sketching on the knowe, one of the legs of Rendall's stool sank into the mound. Carefully removing some of the nearby stones, Rendall uncovered a staircase leading down into the mound. It is generally agreed that it was built between 200BC and 100BC - possibly on the site of an earlier settlement. Standing around eight metres high with an internal diameter of 20 metres, the broch was a tall, easily-defended tower, surrounded by a series of small stone dwellings. All the dwellings are clearly visible from pathways round the site, with their hearths, dressers and bed spaces and toilets with a drainage system, and a spring-fed water tank, and would probably have housed about 40 families.

We stopped for a light lunch at the *Standing Stones Hotel*, before visiting the Stones of *Stenness* and the impressive *Ring of Brodgar*, a mostly intact henge and standing stones, in which (unlike Stonehenge) we were free to walk around, touch and enjoy.

The two sets of stones lie at the north and south extremes of a causeway between two lochs, one fresh water and the other a sea loch, and between the two lies a mound shaped like the back of a whale, which was always thought to be a natural structure until a tooled stone was turned up by a plough in 2003. Geophysical studies then revealed a massive site with multiple buildings, some with walls 15m thick, and the ongoing excavation has found a settlement quite unlike anything else ever found from the Neolithic era. It has been the subject of several television documentaries, and the find is said to have changed radically our understanding of life in those times. In particular, this is the first evidence of a communal site, and has been described as a temple or cathedral. Remarkably some of the finds include a colourfully painted wall, and small thumb pots which may have held pigments, a very early use of such materials. Cate thought the site was like something between a Neolithic craft fair or Ideal Homes Exhibition! The excavation is still in progress, though there was no digging that day as it was Sunday, but we had a most informative and very detailed demonstration of the various structures from one of the archaeologists involved (unfortunately in the rain!) - a brilliant end to a fascinating day. Kinlay returned us to the marina after a tour that lasted almost 8 hours, much longer than we had expected, and above our agreed time. We are most grateful to Kinlay, and would certainly recommend his tours to anyone[14].

It was back to the *Ferry Inn* that evening for more Olympics and good pub grub.

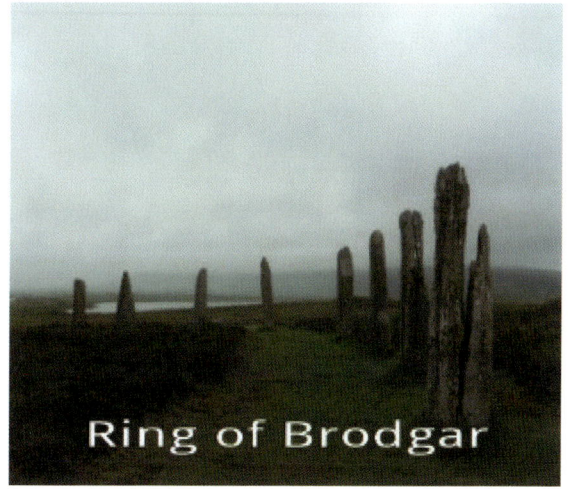

Ring of Brodgar

---

[14] Kinlay's company is here *https://orkneyuncovered.co.uk/*

Monday: Kirkwall

We caught the bus to *Kirkwall* to see *St Magnus Cathedral* and the *Earl's Palace*, and check out the town and shops. We started with a coffee at *Reels*, a super wee cafe which specialises in traditional Scottish music, with its own regular music school run by the Wrigley Sisters (fiddle and guitar), but of course in accordance with the ever-reliable *Benjamin's Law*, music in pubs etc is always yesterday or tomorrow! We did the shops (Cate finding more *Ronaldsay* wool, and Benj a limited edition *Highland Park* malt), then the cathedral and palace. St Magnus is as magnificent as any European renaissance cathedral, with towering pillars and beautiful stained glass windows, the stone tomb of the explorer John Rae, complete with rifle and bible, and a Poets' corner with plaques to *Mackay Brown* and *Edwin Muir*. It dates from the bloody years of the 12th century, when feuding between earls resulted in the slaying of *Earl Rognvald*'s uncle *Magnus* on the orders of his cousin *King Haakon*, and the site became a place of pilgrimage.

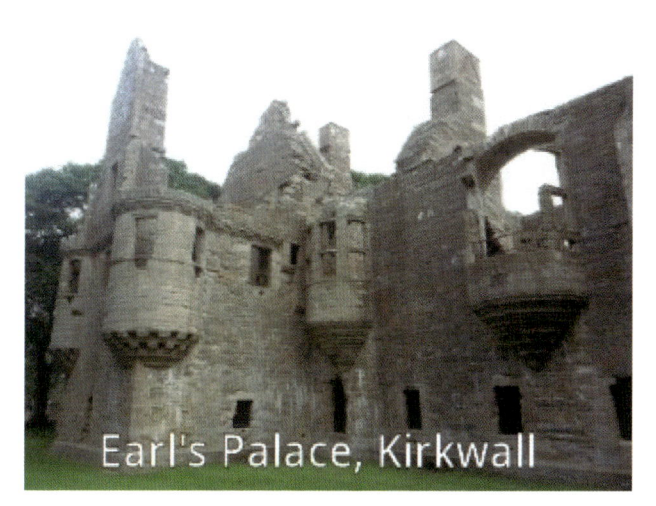

The *Earl's Palace* is a splendid ruin, with good information boards. Its builder was an infamous earl who used forced labour in the construction, but was eventually besieged and overthrown by the Earl of Caithness, and hanged for treason.

Earl's Palace, Kirkwall

We caught the bus finally southwards towards *Burra* and South *Ronaldsay*, crossing the causeway barrier protecting one inlet to *Scapa Flow*, to visit the *Italian Chapel*. The causeway was built with the labour of some 1200 Italian POWs who were housed in Camp 60 on the island in WW2, and they constructed a chapel using two Nissen huts end to end, concrete, barbed wire and part of a rusting blockship. It was decorated inside by *Domenico Chocchetti*, and has the most exquisite tromp-l'oeil wall paintings. Mass is still celebrated there regularly. We caught the bus all the way home to *Stromness* and dined aboard, ready to resume our cruise the next day.

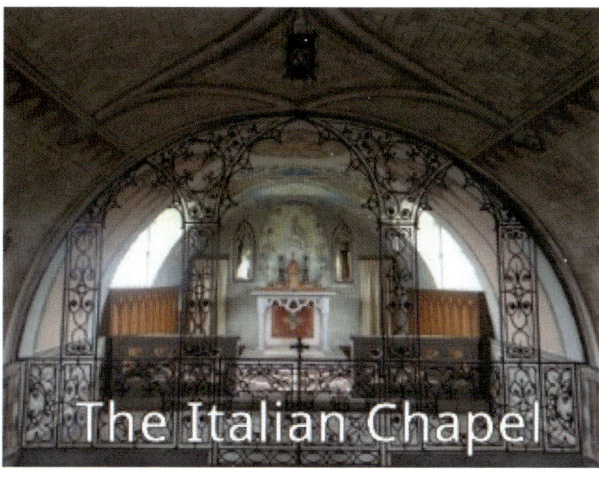

The Italian Chapel

Day 84 Tue 7 Aug
Stromness to Wick
Lat: 58:26.38N Lon: 3:05.06W

(In which Vega crosses the dreaded Pentland Firth without a hitch)

Farewell to Orkney

This would be a potentially scary passage, crossing the notorious *Pentland Firth*, the almanacs and cruising manuals awash with warnings to vessels large and small about the overfalls, high seas and ferocious tidal streams of 9knots or more. Careful study of the charts and pilotage books suggested that a plan to leave around 0700 would catch the right tide (this time) round *Hoy* Sound and down between the islands of *Graemsay, Cava, Rysa* and *Flotta,* and round *Cantrick Point* and then meet the crucial east-going tide through the Firth. Just to cross check, I had called Shetland Coastguard the night before to discuss the plan: they left me on hold for a while, and came back to say we must be at *Swona* by 1000 to get the tide right. In fact the plan worked out well (though – *Benj True Confession* here - I was half an hour out because I had got the date wrong on my watch - duuh!) and we were indeed west of *Swona* at 1000, and began to pick up the tide, which whisked us along at almost 10k over the ground, with a calm sea and remarkably little swell in the 3-4knots of wind. As a result we rounded *Duncansby Head* and *Noss Head* and were tied up in *Wick* marina at 1300.

Wick town and harbour, formerly Scotland's principal herring fishing port, has seen better days and is rather sad and run down despite the town's obvious best efforts at rejuvenation. The marina itself is pretty new and well-found, though the facilities are rudimentary - one end of a fish shed with a single rather grubby shower and a sign saying there are plans to

Isabella Fortuna, 1898, Wick

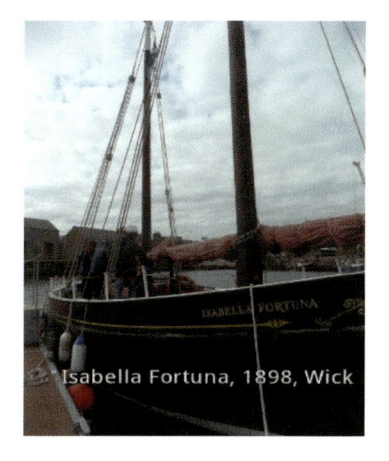

upgrade in 2010! We walked into town, which was equally shabby, a great shame since it was once one of *Thomas Telford's* finest achievements in town planning, but has clearly never recovered from the loss of the fishing industry. Cate found a wool shop (of course!) and Benj hiked to Tesco on the edge of town for essentials, and we met up at The *Alexander Bain*, a *Wetherspoon* pub. (Bain was the inventor of the first electronic character transmitter, the fore-runner of the fax machine.)

Benj just managed to scrape into the Wick Heritage Centre as they were closing, and was given generous time to walk round the huge and comprehensive collections. There are exhibits of everything from fishing boats, rescue equipment, the original Noss Head light, reconstructions of homes from the 19th and early 20th centuries, a cooperage (barrels used for the herring), history of photography and printing presses, fish smoking, and Caithness glass. The photograph collection belongs to three generations of a family photographic business and is a remarkable record of life in and around the town over more than 150 years. LS Lowry painted in Wick, and there are reproductions of two of his pictures, depicting street scenes in his characteristic 'stick man' style. Altogether a deservedly award-winning collection.

Back in the marina Benj went to look at a lovely remnant of the old sail fishing fleet, Isabella Fortuna, built in 1888, and now taking visitors out for trips round the bay. The weather was now settled dry enough to complete a repair to our deckhouse hatch, whose metal runner had come adrift, requiring complete removal (hence the need for a dry spell) and some minor surgery, while Cate did some housework below decks. We also deflated and stowed the dinghy, as we doubted we would need it for some time, so avoiding prolonged towing. After all that it was time for supper, and as Tuesday is Steak Night in Wetherspoons we returned there and ate while Brazil beat Korea 3-0 in the Olympic semi-final.

WEEK TWELVE
8th – 14th August
Wick to Whitby

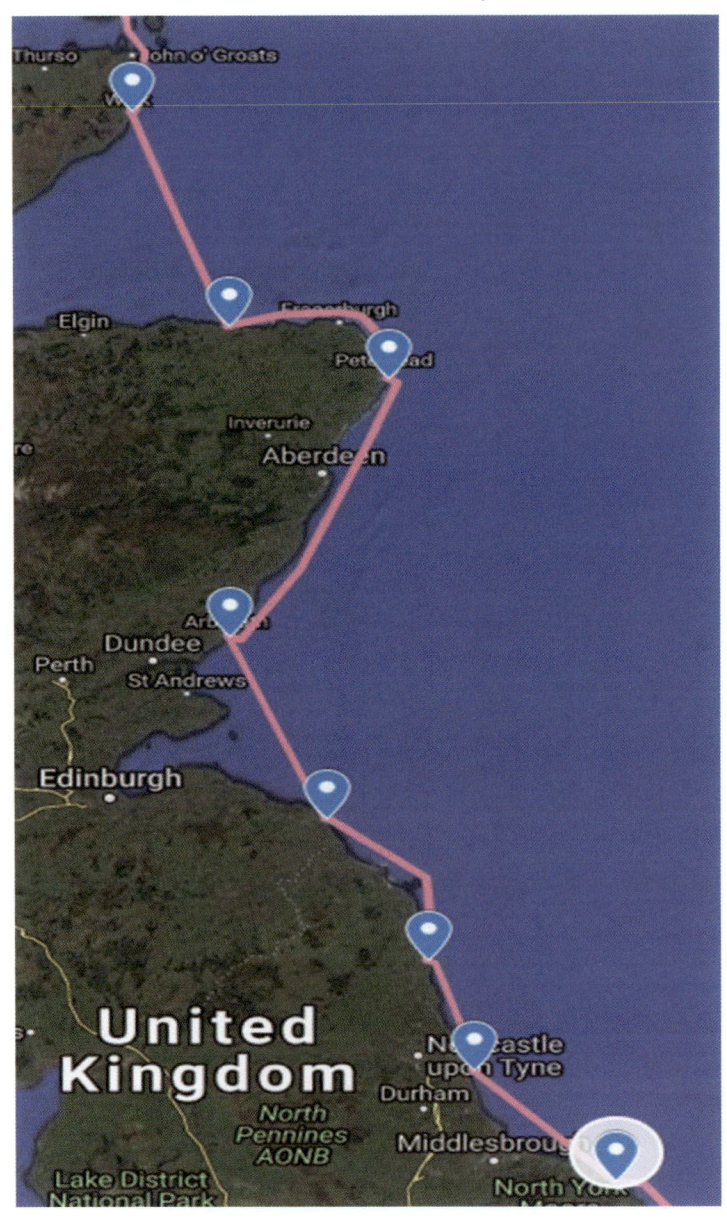

Day 85 Wed 8 Aug
Wick to Whitehills
Lat: 57:40.80N **Lon:** 2:34.90W

(In which Vega starts her race home down the east coast.)

This was to be the first of a sequence of early starts, as we were now aware we were approaching borrowed time. Back home, Benj's daughter *Lucy* has sold her home, bought a property to let in Gillingham, and their household was packed and despatched to Oz, Cate's son *Leigh* and his wife *Ale* have found a house to rent in Deal, and Professor Benjamin's tolerant colleagues at the *London Deanery* were pressing him for dates in September when he might consider doing some actual work! We had done our best not to let the need to make progress more important than taking time and having fun, but we were now effectively 'passage making'. Accordingly we left at 0615, now still firmly in the centre of a large high pressure system, with not a breath of wind, so thank God for Mr Volvo and his reliable *D1-30* engine, which got us to *Whitehills* by 1515, straight onto the fuel berth for 86litres of red diesel.

(Digression on the Red Diesel Saga: in 2012, UK sailors were well aware of the fuss over the use of marked diesel in leisure craft, now prohibited under EU law, but ignored by the British authorities, not least for the practical reason that most harbours only have red diesel, intended for commercial vessels, at the lower duty rate. However, Belgian authorities had now been boarding boats passing through their waters, checking the tanks for red fuel, and either fining the skipper or impounding his boat, irrespective of receipts etc. So marinas began to sell the red fuel to yachts as 60:40 - 60% for 'heating' at the lower rate and 40% for propulsion - notwithstanding the fact that *Vega's* diesel heater has not worked for over a year. Thank you, EU! Digression ends.[15])

Whitehills has a rather tricky entrance, round two tight right angled turns, but a very sheltered harbour, shared by fishing boats, resident yachts, and one pontoon for visitors, which was full (6 boats) by the late

---

[15] At the time of editing (November 2020) this issue has still not been resolved, and it is unclear how Brexit will make a difference. The timeline and current position is summarised here https://www.crownoil.co.uk/news/sailors-to-be-consulted-over-uk-pleasure-craft-red-diesel-ban/

evening. We had excellent and friendly assistance from the harbourmaster with the diesel, for which we had to pay cash, as the harbour does not stretch to a card machine. The HM said we could get cashback at the local (only) shop, which we did, and we set off for the restaurant above the *Cutty Pub*, as advised in the books. It has been closed for many months, but we had a beer in the pub, and went in search of the *Seaford Hotel*, to find it too has been closed for a couple of years! So that is it for *Whitehills* - one pub, one shop, one fish and chip shop (excellent) which we sampled that night. Yet another old established fishing port in decline.

Day 86 Thu 9 Aug
Whitehills to Peterhead
Lat: 57:29.80N Lon: 1:46.42W

(About which there is little more to say)

Slipped the berth in a bright yellow sunrise, through the chicane of the harbour entrance, and headed east with a ghost of tide following (no wind of course). The tide continued to pick up nicely for us, and we turned southeast round *Rattray Head* at 1140, another of the great headlands of the UK coastline, keeping a respectful 2 miles off to minimize the usual overfalls found around all the headlands. We averaged a touch over 6k and were in *Peterhead* at 1430, passing through the massive commercial harbour with tankers and oil rig vessels, onto a quiet berth just inside the entrance to the very large marina. The office would be unmanned until 1600, so we just chilled aboard in a pleasant afternoon sun. (Note: last time here, in 2008, with Cate and long-standing shipmate *Nick Cavell*, we met *Rob Smith*, the BBC News presenter, on his solo circumnavigation, raising funds for charity, and loaned him our facilities key, as he had arrived late! Also in 2008, it was from here, via bus to *Aberdeen*, that both Nick and Cate left for Deal, and *Clive Metcalf*, local Deal artist and musician manqué, had joined me for the onward passage south). We decided there wasn't much need to make the long hike into town, so we dined aboard and spent a restful night, overlooked by the huge towering oil tanks and cranes of this busy oil terminal. Nothing more to say.

Day 87 Fri Aug 10
Peterhead to Arbroath
Lat: 56:33.22N Lon: 2:34.99W

(In which we learn of a sinking at sea, but fail to get a Smokie)

Slipped at 0605 and crossed the quiet harbour shaping up for a long 65nM passage to *Arbroath*. The first half of the journey was again windless, and although we would have had just enough breeze towards the end to get us there, we believed we would by then miss the tidal gate for the entry to the harbour. We later learned from the HM that the 'bar' at the entrance had been dredged long ago, and apart from a fairly short period with gates shut, and a low sill at the entrance, the constraints are not now really troublesome. Nevertheless, we motored on, passing *Slains Castle*, dodging BFSs off *Aberdeen* harbour, with at least 16 boats at anchor, and the city of *Montrose*. We saw several dolphins, and also wondered at strange flocking behaviour of gulls and shearwaters, apparently attending major avian conventions of some importance, crowding together by the hundreds, but not apparently feeding. Wish we were better informed ornithologists! (Where was the aforementioned *Clive Metcalf* when we needed him?) At 1545 there was the start of VHF traffic on ch16, with a *Mayday Relay* call for a fishing vessel, *Audacious*, about 60M east of *Aberdeen*, sinking with 6 crew aborting to liferafts. Two helicopters and the *Hartlepool* lifeboat were despatched, but we heard no more after that, and oddly, the HM in *Arbroath* knew nothing of a sinking fishing boat. Why this type of boat would sink 60M offshore in fine weather is a puzzle, unless they hit a stray container under the waterline or similar. The reason for the sinking at that time remained unclear but has since been the subject of a maritime enquiry. [16]

---

[16] The MIA enquiry concluded that 'a failure of the seawater cooling system was the likely cause. …An alarm activated in the wheelhouse but this went unnoticed at an early stage because the wheelhouse was unmanned for a period.' It is fortunate that there was no loss of life.

Ninety-nine Days

At 1850, 65nM from our start, we were on the hammerhead in *Arbroath*, where we were greeted by the HM, with a key for the facilities and the information mentioned above about the dredging of the entrance, and that the gates would open again at 0715 next morning. We considered refuelling on our way out the next day, but we didn't at all like the look of the wall we would have to tie up to, so we decided it could wait until the next harbour! Sadly, the shop/stall that sells the famed *Arbroath Smokies* was closed (again – just like in 2008!), so we never did get a chance to have one fresh. We made do with the local pub and more Olympic action instead.

An example of the smokies we never managed to get!

Day 88 Sat Aug 11
Arbroath to Eyemouth
Lat: 55:52.50N Lon: 2:05.29W

(In which we reach our last port in Scotland, making good progress southwards.)

Eyemouth harbour

Left on the 0715 gate opening promptly, and reported our passage plan to *Forth* Coastguard, who informed us there was force 5/6 off *Fife Ness*, to which we were intending to give safe clearance anyway. (Digression on passage plans: we are all supposed to report our planned passages and ETA to the relevant Coastguard, though many, maybe most, don't bother. We have been somewhat inconsistent, but do report the longer passages or those with known hazards or in severe weather. However, I (Benj speaking here) am prone to the cardinal sin of forgetting to report arrival at the destination after a long passage, and wonder what the coastguards do with the half-reports of all those miscreant sailors missing presumed lost at sea! It would be more to the point to do the other thing we are supposed to, which is to let *someone at home* know the plan, as they are more likely to worry for our safety if they hear nothing at the end of the trip, but we never do that either! Smacked wrists. End of digression!)

Eyemouth harbour

We rounded *St Abb's Head* in a freshening SE wind (ie, on the nose as usual), and crossed the wide opening of the *Firth of Forth* with hazy views of the *Isle of May* to starboard, thinking how nice it would have been to put into *Port Edgar* and spend a week at the *Edinburgh* Festival, just about to start: note in the diary for another year maybe?

The wind strengthened and the sea became decidedly rough rather than moderate as we progressed, and by 1500 it was F5+ and very lumpy indeed. Reaching *Eyemouth* we followed the leading marks into the entrance, lining up two orange posts to give a bearing of 175°, and into the shelter of the long narrow harbour. There is a long pontoon on the south side, and there was an inviting space (the only one) in front of *Martha*, a 30ft yacht with an enthusiastic sailing couple from *Tayport* who were also heading south. The HM met us and gave us directions to the facilities, which proved to be of a very high standard, housed in a modern building next to the fishing basin and ice making plant. The view across the harbour to the Maritime Museum and bars opposite had the look and feel of a Dutch port about it, the truncated sign of the *' hip Inn'* prominent, with its neighbour *'The Contented Sole'*. We did the tour of the eating options, and avoided a loud party in the *' hip'*, opting for a meal at a comfortable if bland modern bistro.

Day 89 Sun 12 Aug
Eyemouth to Amble
Lat: 55:20.37N **Lon:** 1:34.25W

(In which we enter England, get help with our crossword, and close the Olympics.)

Seals at play, Eyemouth

Lindisfarne (Holy Isle)

Bamburgh Castle

Left at 0700, past seals cavorting in the harbour entrance, lining up the orange markers again in reverse, and turning southeast for a close coastal passage. At 0925 we passed *Berwick-on-Tweed*, which meant we have left Scotland, and we texted friends and families to tell them so. Soon after we passed *Lindisfarne* (*Holy Island*) with hazy views of the monastery, then inshore of the *Farne Islands* and past the huge *Bamburgh Castle*. Once again the wind got up and the sea became heavier with an unpleasant swell, enough to make us wonder why we do it! Approaching *Amble*, I was concerned about our clearance with tidal height over the sill at the harbour entrance, so called the HM on VHF. He said we would have to hurry to make it, so we gunned our reliable Volvo and actually entered the harbour with just above 2metres of water (we need over 1.7 to be sure of avoiding a grounding). I had requested to start at the fuel pontoon, and our man was there to greet us, take our lines, and fill us up - 80litres, meaning our tank had been down to about 20litres.

(Note: we are lucky that our engine is very economical, using about 1.7 litres per hour, so in practice with a full tank we could motor gently for more than 4 days without refuelling if we had to.) We were directed to a nice berth, where our man met us again, and we saw him again in the office: he was a very pleasant, albeit extremely garrulous, chap, full of useful advice about the various shallow areas on the way out of the harbour, and our earliest safe exit time the next day (probably about 1000 - music to Cate's ears!). He also advised us which pub would be best to go to, preferably avoiding the High Street, which did indeed seem to be fairly rough, with rather ugly 'yoof' much in evidence. We found the *Wellwood*, which was fine, and ate there (chowder and sausage and mash) and watched the amazing Olympic closing ceremony almost to the end on a large screen. Even there the clientele were a little odd: one strange man repeatedly introduced himself to us, and gave Cate a neck massage, and another, seeing we were doing the *Telegraph* cryptic crossword as is our habit, said in a broad Geordie accent *'Can I have a look, I'm a reet nosy bugger?!'* (He did actually know his crosswords, and got one clue for us.) Back to bed for a slower start next day.

Day 90 Mon 13 Aug
Amble to Sunderland
Lat: 54:55.23N Lon: 1:21.15W

(In which we make the most of horrible conditions, and are grateful for a safe haven.)

As we were due a late start we fancied a cooked breakfast, and on local advice headed to *Jasper's*, and also did our provisioning at Tesco across the road. At 1020 we set off for *Hartlepool*, a 45nM passage, knowing the conditions were not going to be great. We followed our talkative HM's directions out of the harbour and past the threatening rocks off the shore, motoring inside *Coquet Island* with its impressive lighthouse. Once clear of the hazards we bumped our way southeast, again with a growing sea and strengthening wind, dodging fishing pots, which are plentiful and it always seems to us placed surprisingly far offshore in deep water. Because of the worsening conditions I had set *Hartlepool* as our target, but had waymarked two possible boltholes if things got too rough, *Tynemouth* and *Sunderland*, both with secure harbours, and I called in our passage plan on that basis to *Humber* Coastguard. By the time we reached the huge tanker anchorage off *Tynemouth* (1500) we were already getting tired of the buffeting and Cate was feeling a bit unwell, but we made the decision to press on further. However, by *Sunderland* (1600 hrs and 28nM on) things had changed, and neither of us fancied another four hours of torture, so we called up the harbour and changed course for shelter. As we approached we heard VHF traffic from a very scared sounding skipper of yacht *Tertia* 12M off *Hartlepool* with engine failure, with *Humber* CG coordinating a rescue by lifeboat. Our actual approach to *Sunderland* was itself rather alarming, with enormous waves breaking on the south harbour wall and on rocks to the north, and *Vega* still giving us a bucking bronco ride. Once deep into the very wide outer harbour the worst of it was over, and we were able to wind our way past the boats on residents' mooring buoys, swaying wildly, and round into the shelter of a very smart large marina, where we were directed to a berth. We had tied up and were starting to put the boat back to rights again - lots of loose bits inside had taken flight while at sea - when the HM came down and told us we had been given the wrong berth and would have to move! We did so quickly, with his help taking lines, and finally settled down at around 1800. While enjoying our usual Evening Prayers, we witnessed a disturbing scene of animal cannibalism: two swans stole the carcass of a dead gull from another gull and were tearing it apart with gusto. As far as we are aware, swans are herbivores, so this must be an unusual sight.

Sunderland is an excellent modern marina, with CCTV and electronically controlled gates and very high quality facilities. We climbed a long flight of stone steps to the clifftop road above the marina and scoped out the pubs for our evening meal, but opted for the *Marina Vista*, a modern Italian restaurant on the top floor of the harbour/marina building. We had good pizza, half of Cate's brought back as a takeaway for tomorrow's breakfast or lunch. We had a quick look at the forecast for next day, which looked like more of the same, but I reckoned that at least we could bash through it all and get to *Hartlepool*, only four hours away, so we retired with that plan in mind.

Cate and Irving Benjamin

Day 91 Tue Aug 14
Sunderland to Whitby
Lat: 54:29.65N Lon: 0:36.78W

(In which we make it to one of our favourite spots, and enjoy award-winning fish and chips.)

Benj: when I was still operating, I used to tell my surgical trainees that *'a plan is a very good basis for changing your mind'*. I visited the facilities early and checked the latest weather forecast from the Met Office: this now called for F3/4, sea state moderate, so I was optimistic that we might not have to stop at *Hartlepool* after all, and might make it to *Whitby*. *Whitby* had always been one of the target visits for this trip. We had been there by land a few years ago and really loved the ambience, and our plan was to take a day off here irrespective of the need to get ourselves home on time. So we left the harbour at 0620, with extraordinary rolling surf coming through the entrance, waves still hammering the breakwater and still plenty of rock'n'roll in the sea, though not as bad as yesterday. We were close to *Hartlepool* by 0900, which would be decision time, checked crew strength (well rested and no longer queasy, though not yet up to pizza for breakfast), and called *Whitby* by mobile phone to check our depth for an entry around 1430. HM confirmed we would be OK and also that he would find us a berth, so we pressed on. Visibility was very poor much of the time, and we deployed radar and nav lights, especially rounding yet another crowded anchorage off *Tees* entrance. The wind did freshen up to 22-24k by 1300, enough make our approach to *Whitby* harbour 'interesting', but we were thrilled to see the hazy outline of Dracula's *Whitby Abbey* appearing out of the mist on top of the East Cliff. We had one additional hazard to negotiate: a large cruise ship was anchored right in the fairway to the harbour entrance, and was loading and unloading passengers to go ashore in ribs. We circled round this obstacle, only to be met by a flotilla coming out, with ribs bound for the cruise ship, fishing boats, jet-skis, pleasure craft out for rides round the bay, a fully decked-out pirate galley, and the Captain Cook Experience, a trip in the original *Whitby* lifeboat, crammed with trippers, all watched by huge crowds of holiday makers thronging every inch of the harbour walls in what was now a very pleasant sunny afternoon. Quite a welcome, we thought!

Access to the upper harbour and marina in the *River Esk* is via a swing bridge which opens every half hour for 2 hours either side of high water (1430 today), so we called the bridge and marina (they both communicate on channel 11), and held station mid-river waiting for the 1430 opening, as we watched the throngs of animated day trippers and holidaymakers. There was a real carnival atmosphere, as if the whole world had come to join in the fun. Our HM later said this was just a normal day and we should just wait and see what the mayhem is really like on *Whitby* Regatta weekend, just coming up. The marina is sited on two long pontoons on the west side of the river, and the HM was waiting for us and squeezed us into a rather tight space on the second pontoon. We had made it, the sun was shining, and we were looking forward to a day and a half enjoying *Whitby*. We took a 10 minute walk to the bridge and just made it across to the east side before the 1600 opening, and wandered round the quaint cobbled streets that weave up the hill towards the 199 steps that climb up to the Abbey. Cate found another Wool Heaven - *Bobbins* - so I left her there and continued to browse. The *Captain Cook Museum* was shut, so I earmarked that one for the next day.

Pirates ahoy in Whitby!

We dined royally on fish and chips aboard from one of the several 'Finalists in the Chippy of the Year Competition for 2012': there must be at least 30 chippies in the town! Finally it was nice to retire knowing we did not have to get up early next day, and hoping for more of this warm sunny weather.

Cate and Irving Benjamin

WEEK THIRTEEN
15th – 22nd August
Home strait – Whitby to Deal

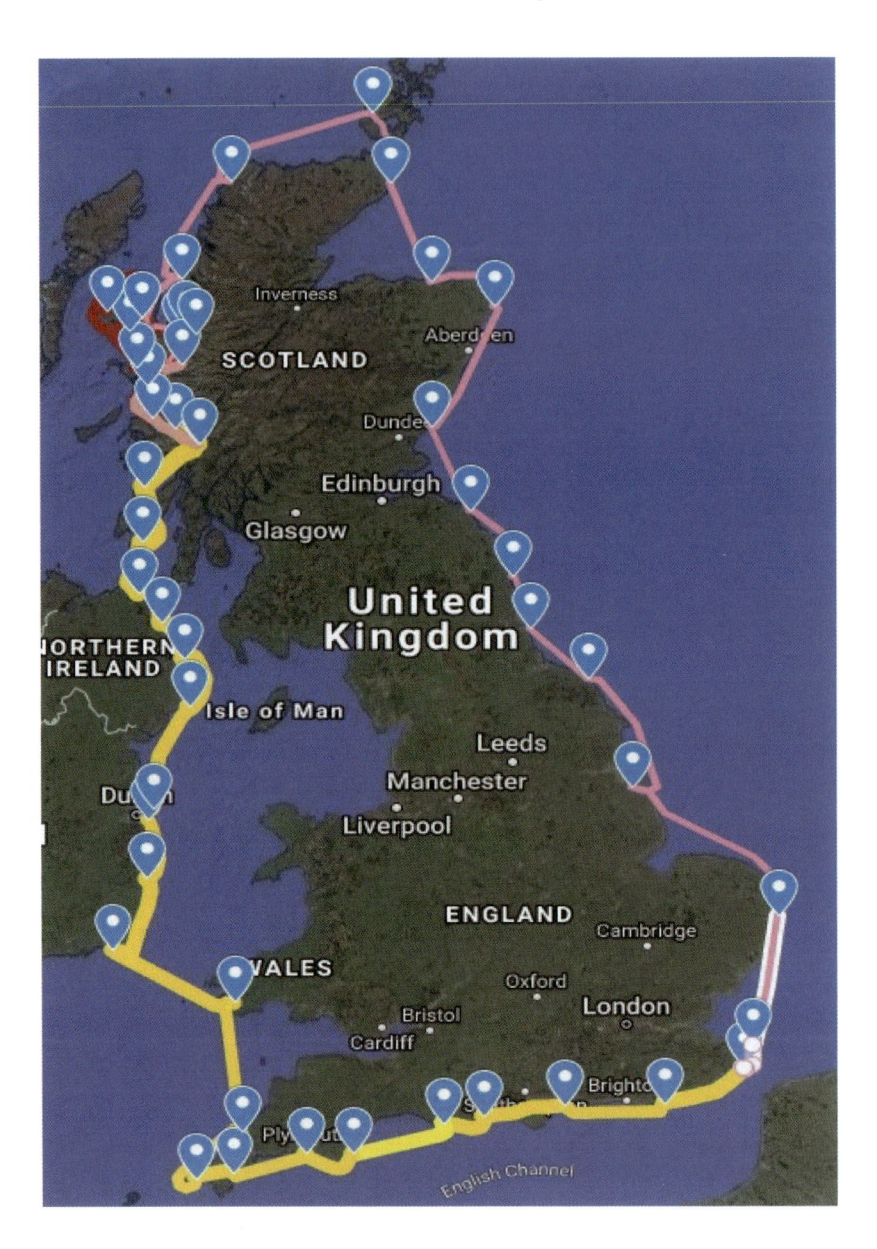

Ninety-nine Days

Days 92-93 15-16 Aug
Getting our teeth into Whitby
(In which we enjoy a day off in Dracula country.)

With the promise of an almost perfect weather day for sightseeing and wandering round historic *Whitby*, we planned to make the most of it with an early start, though we were frustrated by the HM who told us we would have to move the boat, and we rafted outside another small yacht with some complicated warp arrangements. We did eventually get off, and as Benj had underprovided his daily pills (silly old bugger that he is), and would be a week short, he threw himself on the mercies of the *Boots* pharmacist and got some emergency supplies. While Cate was exploring the shops on the west side of the *Esk*, he visited the *Captain Cook Museum*, which was a very well laid out and very informative exhibition, covering Cook's early days as an apprentice to Capt Walker, whose cottage houses the collection, and all his subsequent explorations. There is a lot of detail about the scientific and ethnographic discoveries, with original letters and articles by *Banks* and others, as well as all things nautical. We met up again at the *Dolphin*, and did our crossword outside in the late afternoon sunshine. The plan had been to leave at 0200 on the first bridge opening for what was to be a long overnight passage to *Grimsby*, but a final check on the forecast showed that we must wait another 24 hours to avoid a very bumpy ride with more F6 wind on the button, so we informed the HM and prepared for another night's stay.

The next day (Thursday) Cate had a session at the hairdresser and Benj refuelled the boat from our spare can, and refilled from the pump in the marina, then we met up again and climbed the 199 steps to the *Abbey*. It was another gloriously sunny day, and after wandering round the ruins (with a helpful audio guide courtesy of English Heritage), we sat down against one of the columns and ate crab sandwiches with *Fentiman's* lemonade. As we watched the view across the harbour entrance, we saw a yacht being towed in by the lifeboat - there but for the Grace of God… and God bless the RNLI! I felt rather tense in anticipation of an early start at 0200, and after preparing our lines etc for an easy getaway in the dark, I went to bed to get some sleep, leaving Cate to fill the flasks for the next day, as we'd have no more shore power from now on.

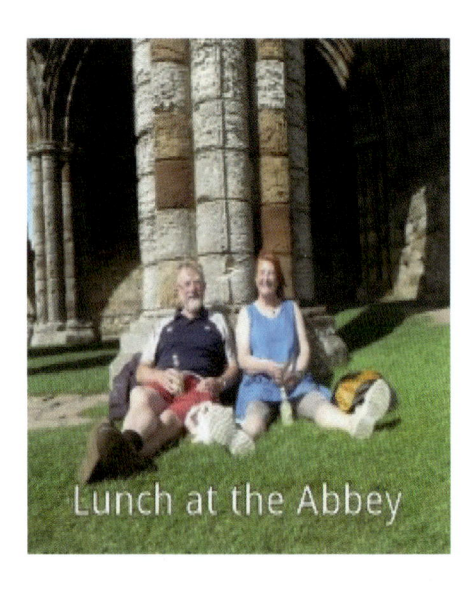

Lunch at the Abbey

Ninety-nine Days

Day 94 Friday 17 Aug
Whitby to Grimsby
Lat: 53°33'20N Long: 0°04'24W

(In which we beat our way through the rough seas in the small hours to reach Grimsby, but without music.)

Up at 0145, anxious that the bridge operator might not turn up for his early shift, and called on VHF11, to be told to call 2 minutes before the 0230 opening time. We cast off into the river, slowly drifted down in the pitch dark toward the bridge, and were mightily relieved when we saw the controller making his way to the road gates! They only open half the bridge unless there is two way traffic, which feels very odd when going through, but works well. We headed out straight into wind as always on the nose, which proved to be between 22 and 32knots all night/day, putting us into the Near Gale range, with towering seas to match. In the latter part of our passage, we heard of two yachts grounded, and the lifeboats deployed yet again: our trip has been punctuated with news of other people's mishaps, which certainly concentrates the mind and engenders respect for the elements. At 0500, off *Scarborough*, we saw the first light of dawn, and Cate took over the watch while Benj caught up on some rest, though real rest was almost impossible with heavy pitching and slamming, enough in the forepeak cabin to lift one bodily off the bed! At 1800 we were off the entrance to the Humber estuary, following the recommended small craft route between the complex shipping lanes. We passed the extraordinary *Tetney Monobuoy*, not a Marvel Comics Superhero but a floating oil terminal with a long fuel pipe snaking out into the waters of the *Humber*. On our way in we passed a BFS refuelling, steadied by a tug astern, but next day on our way out it would have been all too easy, in fog for example, to run over the floating fuel line with Lord knows what consequences! The water was still remarkably rough, and we had our final battle with the 2+knot ebb tide, but we arrived at the lock gate for the *Grimsby* Fish Dock on free flow, and were berthed by 2030.

We made our way to the clubhouse, HQ of the *Humber Cruising Association*, whose guests Clive Metcalfe and I had been in 2008. Sadly, in keeping with *Benjamin's Rule*, their regular members' music night, in which Clive and I had joined for an impromptu gig back then, was yesterday! This is one of the most welcoming clubs I have visited, and has an interesting provenance. A group of sailors, mostly from *Hull*, purchased a part of the disused Fish Dock with their own funds, and fabricated and installed floating pontoons and all the necessary equipment for a sailing club, including comfortable bar and club facilities, and simple but perfectly adequate toilets and showers. The facility is still owned and run by the members for the members. I learned on my last visit that it is now almost impossible to get membership, as they wish to discourage those who would like to join just to use the boatyard facilities, scarce in this area, then leave. The beer remains the cheapest I have ever drunk! After a cleansing ale we retired to recover from our gruelling 19 hour night/day on the North Sea.

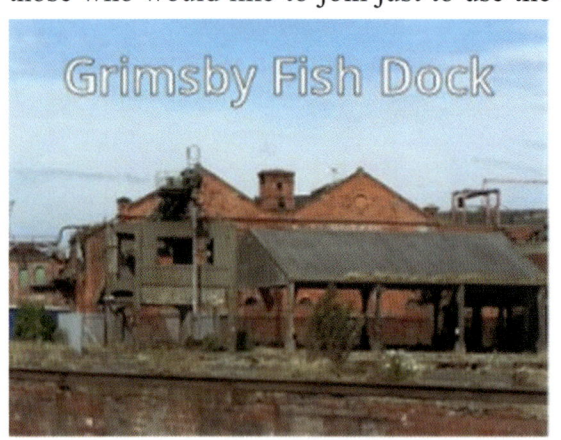

Ninety-nine Days

Days 95-96 Sat 18- Sun 19 Aug
Grimsby to Lowestoft.
Lat: 52:28.31N Lon: 1:45.39E

(In which Benj again enjoys the pleasures of night sailing, and we learn of a possible change of passage plan.)

I (Benj) had previously experienced the town of Grimsby, and was not keen to repeat the experience, so I stayed behind and did our laundry - necessary because we had somehow shipped enough of the North Sea into the forepeak to soak our bedding - while Cate made the long and dismal trek into town, around the derelict fish docks, which look like film sets for gritty and violent British gangland movies. We joined up later, and we bought our provisions in a large modern shopping complex which must have sounded the final death knell to the dying fishing town, as grim as its name. Tidal considerations suggested a departure on the start of the afternoon lock opening (1700), 'punching' the early tide down the *Humber* and catching the good tides round the first corner, and importantly after *The Wash* round the headland at *Cromer*. Most of this worked out well, and the conditions were at last kind to us, and we hoisted the mainsail for the first time in many days, and actually SAILED (!!!) for an hour in the early morning.

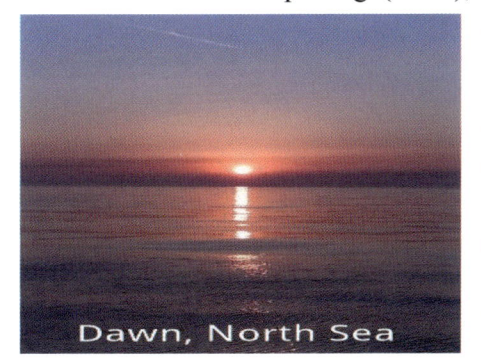

Dawn, North Sea

The stress on this trip of 19 hours was for once not the weather, but difficult light interpretation during the night watch, with VHF messages from a dredger to keep a safe distance, a complicated strange object moving slowly on our course whose identity I (Benj) still have no idea about, a long tug-and-tow running on our course, and a massive wind farm casting bizarre radar shadows. Set against that was the most extraordinary clear starry night sky, and magnificent sunset and dawn, and amazing dazzling dayglow green phosphorescence sparkling in our wake. At times I briefly turned off our nav lights and covered the screen of the plotter to get total darkness, and using the Google Sky app on my Galaxy tablet, I identified stars, including *Vega* directly overhead, and watched *Venus* rising over the eastern horizon while *Jupiter* shone brightly ahead of us. It is experiences like these which make all the difficulties worthwhile. By 0600 we were enjoying beautiful warm sunshine and a steady F3/4, with no engine noise, and in shorts and T-shirts eating our breakfast rolls, but by 1000 the wind was gone, and we motored into *Lowestoft* at midday.

We refuelled before berthing and paid our dues at the magnificent 1903 building which houses the *Royal Norfolk and Suffolk Yacht Club*, the most easterly yacht club in Britain. We sat outside and Benj enjoyed a pint of ale from the local *Tom Thumb* brewery. (Benj - as an aside, I really wish I had catalogued all the different ales I sampled during the cruise - I started well, but didn't continue, so the only evidence I have now is in my sadly expanded waistline!) We met friends Jim and Janet from the Wellington Dock in *Dover* on our pontoon, in their motor cruiser *Idle Hours*. They had arrived on a straight run of 88nM all the way from *Dover*, going outside the complex sandbanks and channels of the Thames Estuary, which gave me pause for thought: we need not actually do as planned and stop two nights at some of the east coast harbours, and could knock days off our passage home. (Of course, Jim did his passage in four hours, his motor boat planing at 20kn, but each to his own!). We had a superb meal of seabass fillets at the Yacht Club, and retired, Benj staying up a little later to revise the final passage plans.

Day 97 Mon 20 Aug
Lowestoft
Lat: 52.28.31 N **Long**: 1.45.39 E

(In which we enjoy our last 'foreign' port, watch a movie and meet an eccentric mariner.)

Gentle rise and shower and Benj off to town across the lifting bridge in search of the chandlery to buy Imray Chart C1 for the new passage plan south to Kent and home (strange to be lacking the one chart so close to home!). Found the very small shop with directions from a retired fish gutter, and got both chart and East Coast Pilot, then parted company with Cate, bound for the shops, and returned to the RNSYC for a coffee and use of the WiFi. Incidentally, the Yacht Club is one of the more splendid examples of the species, with a long history and associations with many illustrious sailors, impressive cabinets of silverware and a formal dress code required in the Members' Bar in the evenings. We were pleased to see an RCPYC pennant hanging in the lounge. Reunited for lunch at the *Harbour Inn* (good butternut squash soup, and very disappointing scallops), then home to do the chartwork. I had found there is a tiny cinema near the marina, showing *The Bourne Legacy*, so booked for the 2000 show. While we were having EPs, we were approached by a wiry sailor in his 60s from *Evergreen*, a Freedom 27 berthed behind *Vega*, asking for information about *Dover*. He was in need of a Tiller Pilot for his onward journey, though on further discussion it was strange he had not had one long ago: he had sailed his little craft (not in the best of nick to our casual inspection) from Poland, via Sweden and Denmark, single handed with no autohelm, snatching 5 minutes sleep from time to time in storm conditions through the North Sea oilfields. We invited him aboard for a beer and heard his story. He is a Czech national who was relocated with his wife and children in 1985 as a refugee, sent to Australia, where he worked as a computer technician. However, he has spent most of the intervening years, sailing and doing boat deliveries all over the world, including Malaysia, the *'Caribbic'* (he spoke in broken English), Venezuela and almost anywhere else you can name. We gave him advice and information about *Dover* and where he might get his Autohelm, and the new genoa he also needs, exchanged email addresses, and told him to be sure to visit the RCPYC in *Dover*. It was clear from his questioning that he knew absolutely nothing of UK ports, and it turned out he has no almanac and only electronic charts, so we donated him our UK marina guide, which he accepted reluctantly! Off to the truly miniscule *East Coast Cinema,* where we watched (er, I slept through) the *Bourne Legacy* with 4 other customers. On the way back there were still young kids playing in the illuminated fountains in the pleasant square outside the yacht club and Family Fun arcade, running around, screaming with delight and enjoying getting soaked in the warm evening. Off to bed, where Cate explained the plot of the movie to me, and a good night's sleep ready for almost our last lap, starting at 0700 the next day.

Day 98 Tue 21 Aug
Lowestoft to Ramsgate
Lat: 51.336°N Long: 1.416°E

(In which we make it across the Thames Estuary to our final stop.)

With our new passage plan worked out and marked on chart and plotter, Benj rose at 0530, showered, filled the thermos flasks[17] and prepared for departure. We were out of the harbour by 0700, into hazy sun with early mist obscuring the horizons. Once we had cleared the offshore shoals we turned onto our course for the North Sunk marker, the first of several which would have us skirt closely by the various complex traffic lanes in the southern North Sea, avoiding all the sandbanks of the Thames Estuary by going outside them. Most of the course, from 0730 to 1400, would be virtually due south, and of course that meant we were pointing head to what wind there was (in fact less than 5k at the start and about 14k at the end) so another day's motoring. The good news is that the planned tidal calculations worked out perfectly, and we were doing over 8k with up to 3k of helpful tide until almost 1500, and the sea state was smooth. Because of the way the very busy shipping lanes in and out of London, *Harwich* and *Felixstowe* work, we had to keep very careful watch with a combination of radar and *Mark One Eyeball*, but in fact there was amazingly little traffic

Approaching Ramsgate

---

[17] I have commented on the thermos flasks several times, but they are worthy of a note. Boiling water on the stove in a boat on rough sea is neither fun nor safe, so whenever we have the opportunity before leaving a secure berth we fill two large thermos flasks (ours have taps to pour from), and we can then enjoy hot drinks throughout most passages. Especially welcome on a night sail. It may seem obvious, but we commend the practice most highly.

around throughout. We passed between huge wind farms, including the *London Array*, still under construction, which is over 8 miles square and our local one off Thanet, a mere 6 miles. We settled into our most common positions for this type of passage, with Cate in the pilot seat watching the horizon and radar while making large advances in her complicated *Gansey* knitting patterns, and I stretched out in the cockpit in the warm sun, finishing my current reading book, with interruptions for the hourly chart plots. By 1600 we had more wind on the bow, and quite a bumpy sea, with up to 2k tide against us, and the last few hours, as is often the case, seemed endless. At 1900 we were approaching the fairway to *Ramsgate* harbour, staying on the south side as instructed by Port Control, with a flotilla of small motor vessels charging in ahead of us. We were inside the marina by 2000, and slotted into a rather tight berth next to a Dutch yacht. Our berth for the night cost £26, and we also noted later that the washing machines were £5 and drying £3, all of which struck us as rip-off level, and must come as a shock to the many visitors from Holland who often make this their first port of call when cruising to the UK. As we climbed the steep ramp to the harbour, we marvelled at the cavernous sides of the harbour walls at low water Springs, like being in a huge amphitheatre. We went for a beer to our sailing neighbours, the *Royal Temple Yacht Club,* of which I am an honorary member since my Commodore-ship at RCPYC, and had a nice Thai meal at the restaurant below the club. We called our respective children at home to announce our arrival: tomorrow is homecoming time.

Ninety-nine Days

Day 99 Wed 22 Aug
Ramsgate to Dover - we're Home!
Lat: 51.06.78 Long: 01.19.80

(In which we are welcomed home by all our loving family.)

0900 departure from *Ramsgate* Marina, on a brilliant sunny day, with a 2+ knot following tide and 14+ knots of S/SE wind just far enough off our heading to allow sailing right from the start, close hauled on starboard tack under full main and 2/3 genoa, making 7-8k over the ground. Real sailing for our last day of the cruise! We had hoisted the Saltire and the SA flag on our starboard spreader, to add to the picture we hoped Leigh would be able to get as we passed Deal pier, though in the event we could not sail high enough upwind to get close into the area of the pier to allow good shots. We sailed on past *Deal* (almost in sight of home!), *Kingsdown* and *St Margaret's*, with great views of the White Cliffs, and were making such speed that at 1045 we had our first view of *Dover* Harbour since our departure 99 days before. In fact by 1100 the wind had freshened (as forecast) to 22k and we were over-sailed, so we took in the genoa and motor-sailed on toward the Eastern Entrance. We called Port Control when we were a mile off, with ferries entering and leaving and even beginning to stack inside the outer harbour waiting for their berth. We were told to hang about to the north of the entrance, and while Cate kept us holding station head to wind, I dropped and stowed the main. As soon as we got the word to enter we headed for the inside of the breakwater and I hoisted our 'dressing overall' signal flags fore-and-aft to celebrate our Circumnavigation and we slowly rounded the Prince of Wales Pier, where Lucy, Rob, Grace and Leigh were waiting to record our arrival. We passed *Karibia Breezes*, with Bernard Sealy and crew aboard, and tied up on the crosswall in front of the lifeboat to await the rising tide for the swing of the bridge to enter Wellington Dock.

The family joined us aboard for drinks and nibbles as we waited, and it was nice also be joined by Nick Cavell, who had cycled down to the marina on the chance we could meet up, prompted by our regular blog and Cate's Facebook messages. After half an hour or so the marina control informed us they were about to swing the bridge, Lucy and Rob left, and granddaughter Grace took the wheel to finally steer *Vega* through the gate and onto our own berth - back at last after 99 days and 2148 Nautical Miles. This of course averages only about 21miles a day, so in essence we could have walked round Britain as fast, but it wouldn't have been nearly as much fun! Home now for our first home cooked meal for a while - Leigh's spag bol - amidst a scene of mild domestic chaos with the Furnesses deep in preparation for their departure for Oz in one week from now, and Leigh and pregnant wife Alessandra ready to move to their own rented house close to us in Deal about the same time. Cate cried when she first saw Grace, and as I first wrote this I had just tucked Grace up, recounting my experience of watching Venus and Jupiter on a clear night at sea. We are looking forward now to a night in our own comfy bed and eventually losing the feeling of perpetual motion on land! Back to reality some time soon no doubt, after our Great Big Adventure, and wondering what we can do next year …

Postscript, 2020: we actually only had a couple more fun sailing trips together, to Calais and Boulogne, before the advance of Cate's cancer put a stop to our adventures. But, as Rick (almost) says in *Casablanca* "*We'll always have Orkney*".

And… back to work!

3 months' mail!

Appendices

Biographies

Cate Benjamin was born **Catherine Graham Edwards** in Durban, South Africa, and returned to the UK for her school education. She returned to South Africa in her teens, where she raised her family of four children. She taught pattern making for the clothing industry, often in the townships, in the years of apartheid South Africa. She moved to Deal, Kent, to care for her parents in their last years, and made her final home there. Two of her children settled in Canada, and two in Deal, and her own grandchildren were born in 2012 (Calgary) and 2014 and 2018 (Deal). She and Benj got together in 2002, and married in 2006. She developed breast cancer the next year while sailing in the west of Scotland, and underwent surgery, chemotherapy and radiotherapy. The cancer returned in 2016, and she endured four more years of chemo. A devoted wife, her passions were knitting, travel, music – a veteran of Glastonbury and other festivals – and her family. She passed away quietly in September 2020, in her own home, supported by Benj and her family.

Benj (Irving Stuart Benjamin) was born in Salford, but brought up in Glasgow, where he studied medicine at Glasgow University. He was married first in 1968 to Barbara, with whom he had three children, and now has four grandchildren. He specialised in Surgery, and did his postgraduate training between Glasgow, Cape Town, Oxford, the USA and London. His final appointment in 1990 was as Professor of Surgery and Consultant Surgeon at King's College Hospital, and joint Head of Surgery, King's College London. He specialised in liver and biliary surgery and travelled widely, lecturing and operating in Europe, Australia, South Africa and Japan. After their marriage n 2006, Cate accompanied him on many of his trips. He took up sailing in 1990, did Day Skipper and Yachtmaster exams, and bought their boat *Vega* in 2004. Benj shared Cate's love of music, sang in Rock Choir with her at the O2, and camped at several rock festivals. He was able to care for her throughout her last months at their home in Deal.

Vega, the boat

LM Vitesse 33
Built 1990
LOA (length overall) 9.85m
Beam 3.10m
Draught (fin keel) 1.6m
Displacement 4800kg
Small ships reg no 37535
Sail plan Bermudan sloop, furling Genoa, spinnaker
Sail number 3328
Engine Volvo Penta D1-30 (new engine in 2006)
Prop saildrive

In the 1950s Danish wood-furniture company LM (Lunderskov Mbelfabrik) started incorporating the newfangled fiberglass into its furniture and changed its name to LM Glasfiber. In 1972, the company built its first fiberglass sailboat, the LM27, and over the next 20 years, it built 3,000 boats, most ranging from 24 to 32 feet, mostly with canoe sterns, some long keel and some fin. They are still popular in Scandinavia. In 1995, LM stopped building boats and claims to be the world's largest maker of the blades for wind farms.

The *LM Vitesse 33* is a sailing vessel with a deckhouse saloon, and so is classified as a 'motor-sailer', but this description in no way implies any lack of performance as a leisure yacht. Yachting Monthly in the 1990s made a head-to-head comparison with a *Sigma 33*, a popular cruising and racing yacht, and the LM stood up well in terms of overall performance. Because she is a heavy boat she is much slower from a standing start, and also fell behind in light airs. However, once she is moving, and with a good breeze, the boat can pick up a good turn of speed, and in the test gave the *Sigma* a run for her money. Handling is excellent, responsive and light on the tiller, and the boat points fairly high into a good wind. We sailed with main (the original one we bought) and a Genoa with a 140 ratio, purchased in 2008. We never used the spinnaker (cowards!).

Steering by wheel inside the deckhouse provide comfortable dry(-ish) motoring in the conditions frequently encountered around Britain, and especially in the West of Scotland. The wheel can be driven by an Autohelm (*Otto* as we called him) which is reliable enough to allow a relaxed long spell of motoring or motorsailing, but as we have no windvane steering, it will allow for changes of tides and currents, but can't compensate for wind changes. Still, *Otto* was a particular boon during night transits, and made for pleasant and easy overnight passages.

Standard equipment in the deckhouse includes VHF radio, Raymarine and Autohelm wind and log instruments. We had a Simrad CX-44 Chartplotter and radar system (but no AIS recognition) installed in 2005, which can be linked to the Autohelm to set multi-leg courses. We used the C-Map chart cartridges for the whole of the UK, and could also for pre-passage planning on a PC at home with PC-Planner software. Plastimo 4 man liferaft. Two-stroke outboard.

Over the cockpit there is an acrylic canopy (replaced in 2007) which folds away neatly when not in use, and makes a cosy 'extension' in the cool or wet evenings sitting out for 'Evening Prayers'.

Down below there is a forepeak v-berth (I thought it comfortable, but Cate never agreed with me), two single side berths each able to open out to a (small) double, and a starboard side berth aft alongside the engine, which is accessed from behind the pilot seat at the wheel: it looks claustrophobic, but is an fact quite cosy (so I am told!). Separating the forepeak and cabin berths, two folding doors enclose the heads (manual flush) and sink, and could be used as a shower, though we never did. The space should be heated by an Eberspacher hot air system, but we never got it to work. I think it needs to be replaced, but I was too poor (?mean) to do it.

The well-appointed galley is opposite the pilot's steering seat and is above the water level with panoramic views. The sales blurb says *'Life is too short for a galley without a view'*. That one we would agree with.

Overall *Vega* is a great boat with good facilities for long-term cruising for up to four in comfort without any compromise in the fun of leisure sailing.

Ninety-nine Days

Victualling Vega

A copy of the original list, regularly updated. For fun, I have left all the annotations made, in my hand and Cate's, for our various trips.

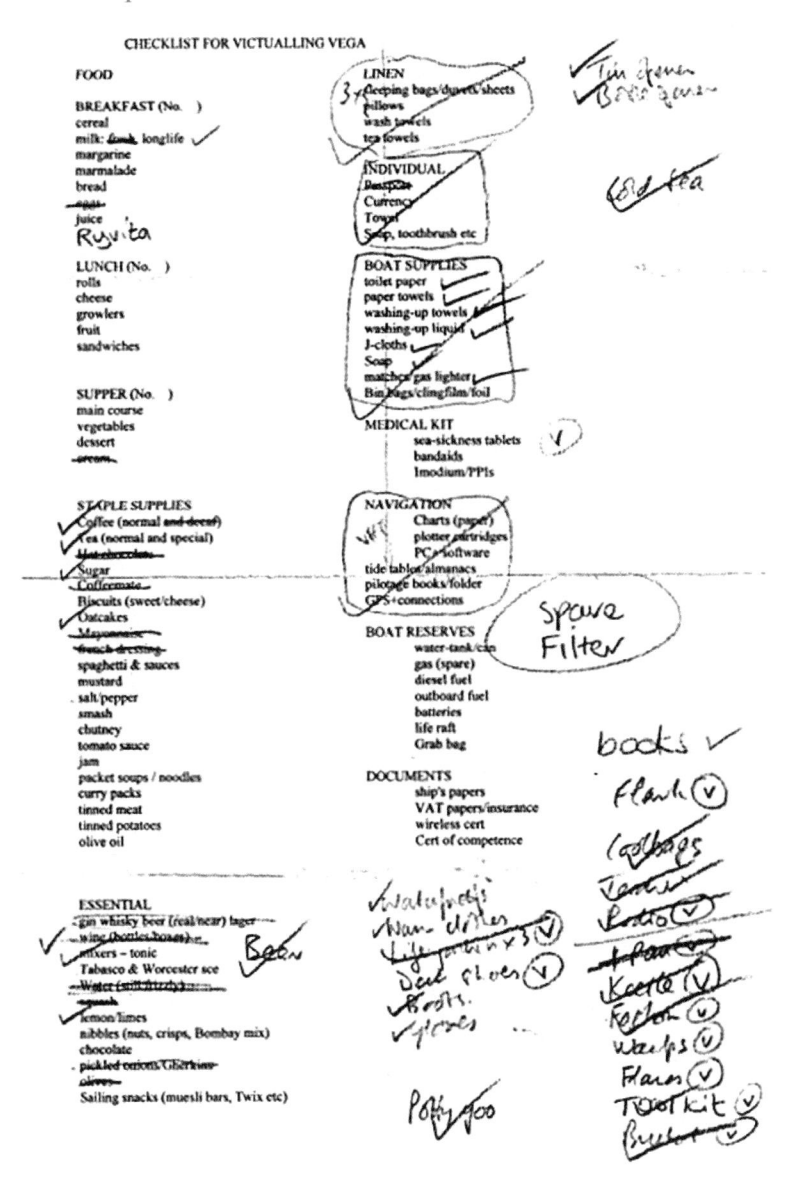

Index of places and people's names

Abbey, 178
Aberdeen, 166
Albastan', 150, 152
Alek, 84
Alexander Bain, 160
Alf Resco, 25
Amble, 170, 172
Anvil Point, 22
Arbroath, 166
Arbroath Smokies, 167
Ardglass, 49, 51, 52, 54, 55
Ardnamurchan, 104
Ardnamurchan Point, 130
Ardnamurchan Point., 103
Ardtornish House, 83
Arklow, 44, 45, 46
Assynt, 146
Aulay's Bar, 88, 96, 98
Avoca River, 45
Ballintoye, 61, 62
Ballycastle, 60, 64, 66, 67, 68
Bamburgh Castle, 170
Bangor, 54, 55, 56, 57, 58
Beachy Head, 20
Belfast, 56, 57
Belfast Lough, 58
Berwick-on-Tweed, 170
Bill Murray, 93
'Blackening', 152
Bloxham, 88
Bloxhams, 90
Bowmore, 72
Bridge, 27
Bridge over the Atlantic, 79

Broch of Gurness,, 155
Bruichladdhie, 74
Burra, 158
Caledonian Hotel, 86
Calgary, 93, 118
Canna, 114
Caol Ila, 117
Cape Wrath, 145, 149
Captain Cook Museum, 175
Carbost, 114
Carnore Point, 44
Cherub, 26
Chichester, 20
Christchurch, 21
Clive Metcalf, 165
Clive Metcalfe, 180
Cloughs, 90
Coastguard, 168
Colonsay, 74, 77, 79
Coquet Island, 172
Cromer, 181
Cuillins, 114
Dark Hedges, 64, 66
Darthaven, 24, 25
Dartmouth, 24, 25
David Clough, 88
David Noble, 96, 102
Deal, 187
Delta Force, 86, 90
Diane, 88
Domenico Chocchetti, 158
Doom Bar, 34, 36, 37
DOOM BAR, 32
Dover, 14, 187

Dows, 86
Dublin, 47
Dun Laoghaire, 49
Duncansby Head, 159
Dunlaoghaire, 46
Dunvegan Castle, 117
Dunvegan Head, 117
eagle, 110
Earl's Palace, 157
Eastbourne, 18
Eddystone, 30
Edinburgh, 169
Edwin Muir, 157
Ee-Usk, 88
Eigg, 104, 105, 107
Eilann Donan Castle, 126
Eyemouth, 170
Fair Head, 60
Falmouth, 30, 31
Felixstowe, 185
Ferry Inn, 150
Fife Ness, 168
Firth of Forth, 169
Flowerdale Falls, 145
Forth, 168
Frankie, 118
Furnesses, 188
Gairloch, 144
gannets, 146
Giant's Causeway, 61, 62
Glasgow, 91, 93, 136
Glenarm, 58, 59, 60
Governor Rocks, 54
Grace, 118, 187
Grimsby, 177, 179
Hartlepool, 166, 172
Harwich, 185

Highland Games, 130, 132
Highland Park, 157
Holy Island, 170
Howth, 49, 51
Howth Yacht Club, 49
Humber, 172, 179
Humber Cruising Association, 180
Iain Dow, 95
Ian Sheldon, 96
Inverie, 109, 126, 129, 130, 138, 140
Irene Clough, 136
Isabel, 94
Isabella Fortuna, 160
Isle of Muck, 58
Italian Chapel, 158
John Bullough, 110
John Clough, 127
Jura, 74
Katie, 118
Kerrera, 79, 91, 100
Kilmore Quay, 41, 44, 46
Kingsdown, 187
Kingswear, 24
Kinlay Francis, 153
Kinloch Castle, 110
Kinlochbervie, 146, 149
Kirkwall, 152, 157
Knitwit', 154
Knoydart, 127
Kyleakin, 122, 124
Kylerhea, 140
Lagavulin, 74
Land's End, 34
Leigh, 187
Lindisfarne, 170

193

Little Minch, 117
Lizard, 32
Loch Aline, 82, 83
Loch Alsh, 126
Loch Dunvegan, 116, 119
Loch Gruinart, 76
Loch Harport, 114, 116
Loch Inchard, 146
Loch Nevis, 130
Loch Snesort, 107
Loch Torridan, 119
London Array, 186
Lorne Bar, 88
Loudons, 86
Lowestoft, 183, 185
Lowry, 160
Lucy, 118, 163, 187
Mackay Brown, 157
Maes Howe, 154
Maiden Island, 82
Mallaig, 130
Malts Cruise, 134
Matthew, 118, 146
Mayday, 166
McGochan's, 103
McGochan's, 130
Mel and Graham, 87
Milford Haven, 37, 39, 41
Mishnish, 103, 130
Montrose, 166
Mosside, 66
Mull, 130
Munro-bagging, 127
Mylor Yacht Haven, 31
Newlyn, 32
Nick Cavell, 165, 188
Noelle, 84

North Ronaldsay, 154
Noss Head, 159
Oban, 79, 82, 85, 88, 93, 102, 132, 136, 137
Old Forge, 126, 127, 128, 138
Old Inn, 114
Old Man of Hoy, 150
Orchestrion, 112
Orkney, 149, 151
Orkney Uncovered, 152
Oronsay, 75, 77
Padstow, 32, 34, 36
Paps, 74
Pendennis Marina, 31
Pentland Firth, 159
Penzance, 32
Peterhead, 165, 166
Plockton, 124, 126, 140, 142
Plymouth, 27
Plymouth Hoe, 28
Plymouth Sound, 27
Poole, 21
Port Ellen, 67, 68, 71, 72, 73, 74
Portland Bill, 24
Portree, 119, 122, 144
Priory, 77
Puilladhobhran, 79
Quaraing, 120
Raasay, 122, 142, 144
Ramsgate, 96, 185, 187
Rathlin Island, 67
Rathlin Sound, 60
Rathlin Sound,, 68
Rattray Head, 165
Red Diesel, 163
Ring of Brodgar, 155
River Esk, 175

Rob, 187
Rob Smith, 165
Ronaldsay, 157
Royal Dorset Yacht Club, 22
Royal Norfolk and Suffolk Yacht Club, 182
Royal Plymouth Corinthian YC, 28
Royal Temple Yacht Club, 186
Rum, 107, 110, 114
Rum orchid, 111
Saucy Mary, 123
Scalsaig, 74
Scarborough, 179
Seil Island, 79
Selsey Bill, 20
Shelley, 98, 113, 114, 119
Skaill House, 154
Skara Brae, 153
Skelmorlie, 136
Skye, 142
Skye Bridge, 122
Slains Castle,, 166
Small Isles, 104
Sound of Islay, 74
Sound of Mull, 82
Sovereign Harbour, 18
St Abb's Head, 169
St Ann's Head, 41
St George's Channel, 39
St Magnus Cathedral, 157
St Margaret's, 187
St Patrick's Bridge', 42
St Patrick's Bridge, 44
St Vincent Crescent, 93

Standing Stones Hotel, 155
Stones of *Stenness*, 155
Storr, 120, 144
Stromness, 149, 151, 159
Sunderland, 172, 173, 174
Susan, 86
Sutherland, 146
Swona, 159
Talisker, 114, 115, 116, 120, 123, 124, 126
Taynuilt, 94
Temple Bar, 47
Tetney Monobuoy, 179
'The Contented Sole', 169
The Minch, 142
The Old Inn, 145
Thomas Telford', 160
Tobermory, 102, 104, 116, 130, 132, 137
Torr Point, 60
Tuskar Rock, 44
Tynemouth, 172
Uist, 114
Ullapool, 142
Waypoint Grill, 80, 96, 100, 136
Wellington Dock, 188
Wemyss Bay, 136
Western Infirmary, 93
Weymouth, 22
Whitby, 174, 177, 179
Whitby Abbey, 174
White Hart Inn, 69
Whitehills, 163, 165
Wick, 159, 163
Woolshed, 154

Printed in Great Britain
by Amazon